PEARSON   ALWAYS LEARNING

Janet Farrell Leontiou, Ph.D.

Communicating With Integrity

Second Custom Edition for Nassau Community College

Cover Art: Courtesy of Amelia Kurpeski

Pearson Learning Solutions, 501 Boylston Street, Suite 900, Boston,
MA 02116
A Pearson Education Company
www.pearsoned.com

Printed in the United States of America

000200010271781030

MM/JG

ISBN 10: 1-269-32944-8
ISBN 13: 978-1-269-32944-6

29 2022

In loving memory of Lawrence W. Rosenfield, whose teachings are a part of me.

Table of Contents

in different ways. The word theory comes from the Greek *theoros* meaning to see.

Information versus A Way of Being

This book is written from a rhetorical perspective. The word rhetoric means many things to many people. The way that it is frequently used within the popular culture is not accurate. Many people use it to mean empty words and that is not what it means. This erroneous understanding of the word rhetoric goes as far back as Plato. There is a long history as to why Plato put rhetoric down but one key reason is that he did not have much confidence in people's ability to talk and think critically after his teacher, Socrates, was tried, found guilty, and killed.

Rhetoric, at the center, means the ability to persuade. I mean persuasion in a grander sense than how we usually use that word. In this book, I will speak about how all words are persuasive. The words we use create a particular world—a symbolic world and we use words to ask others to buy into the world we are creating. Many times, I will use the phrase: a choice of words is a choice of worlds and this is what I mean. The important thing to remember is that we create worlds when we talk. We think that we are just describing what we see and experience. We forget that we are making a choice and that choice affects how we see the world. I will explain more of this perspective later but I wanted to introduce it early since it is a key component of the book.

Interpersonal versus Intrapersonal

Interpersonal communication takes place between me and another person whereas intrapersonal communication takes place within myself. My thinking is that we need to learn about ourselves before we can begin to learn about others. This book asks you to go inside yourself before you focus your gaze outside of yourself. I find that we as a culture do not have much practice with introspection (looking within). When I assign papers, I ask that they be written in first person (language of I). We are trained to speak using the plural we. Some teachers never permit their students to use the language of I when writing a paper. They think that this language is not academic. I think that this is a mistake. The language of I is the language of responsibility. I think that the student needs to understand himself or herself first before they can make sense of the larger world. Research is meaningless unless you first understand yourself.

I think that other cultures may have understood this concept better. Plato (who attributes the expression "Know thyself" to Socrates within the dialogues) talks of the importance of self knowledge but we do not frequently give students an opportunity where this knowledge may be actualized. Socrates's words, then, become empty cliché. A cliché is a well-worn expression but it really means that we use words without thinking what they mean.

Socrates actually provides us with an excellent model for a way of coming to know ourselves. Socrates believed the following: the admission of ignorance is the beginning of all knowing, the power of the spoken word, the creative aspect of talk, and asking insightful questions is more important than arriving at the correct answer. The story is that Socrates went to the Oracle of Delphi and asked who was the wisest of all men? The oracle told him that he was the wisest and Socrates responded with disbelief saying that he knew so little. The oracle told him that was why he was wise: because he knew his limitations, he knew his areas of ignorance, and he knew that which he did not know.

It may sound odd to us but when you think about it, it is true. We begin to learn when we have the humility to say: I do not know. There is also something so refreshing and commendable hearing someone say: I don't know. When was the last time you heard anyone in a position of power admit that he or she did not know the answer to a question? This was the courage of Socrates. Socrates also refused to write even though he could. The written word was an emerging technology at the time and Socrates thought that the written word not only took away from the power of the word, but that its use would destroy peoples' memories. I will speak more about this when I talk about orality but he was making a similar argument to those we hear regarding our own use of technology. Socrates's method was to walk around Athens and engage people in conversation. He believed that through talk, one would begin to see things differently. He believed in the creative power of conversation and so do I. You probably do too.

Through conversation, we can begin to see things that we probably never would see on our own. As people would speak, Socrates would ask questions. This technique is sometimes referred to as Socratic method of asking questions. Socrates believed that if he asked good, sincere, authentic questions, speakers would come to understand their own minds much better than if he made assertions. I, too, am a believer in asking questions and I find that most times, we do not ask questions. We are sometimes not even aware that we are not asking questions. I think that schoolteachers should reward the best question that comes up in class instead of giving points for arriving at the correct answer. Sincere, authentic questions are usually a sign that the person is engaging and wondering. Wondering is the beginning of all thought. When you wonder, you start to ask questions. That is why little children ask plenty of questions. Socrates understood, however, the difference between an authentic question and a counterfeit question. You probably know the difference as well because you can feel it and what you can feel is the other's intention. I will talk more about intention when I speak about the self but here I want to stress that sincere, authentic questions aim to understand whereas counterfeit questions are really disguised attempts to send a message instead of receiving one. Counterfeit questions are veiled attempted to control.

Language as a Tool versus Language as Essential to Our Being

Every interpersonal communication text I have seen refers to language as a tool. (They also state that meanings are in people instead of stating that meanings are both in words and in people.) The first thing to understand is that the word tool here is used as a metaphor. The word metaphor comes from the Greek *metaphorein* meaning to move. We learn that metaphors are figures of speech but they also are figures of thought. Metaphors move our thinking from one place to another. When authors state that language is a tool they are stressing the use of language. It also implies that it is something that we can pick up when we need it and put down when it is no longer of use. This is incorrect. We can never

4

step outside of language. The tool metaphor is a reductionistic way of seeing language. I hope that by the end of this book, you will no longer refer to language as a tool. In my teaching, and in this book, I stress meaning. The other reason I do not like the use of this metaphor is because people do not find meaning among their tools.

The word tool also implies a means to an end. I will critique this entire structure of means to an end when I talk about process versus product. Communication is much more than a tool or a means to an end. This language implies that language is a way to connect us to a world that is separate from us. As I previously have stated, we do not describe a world through our words but instead create a world through our words and then forget that it is our creation.

Schools exist only for those who need them and know that they need them.

P.D. Ouspensky

Chapter II
The Difference Between Education and Training

In the previous chapter, I talked about how this book is different in that it is not written from the perspective of social science. It is important to establish these frameworks because I am establishing a way of thinking about the subject matter. In chapter one, I ended with a critique of language as a means to an end. Now I will offer the idea that if one adopts this means to an end mentality, one kills whatever is being treated as a means. If we treat language as a means to an end, we kill language. If we treat education as a means to an end, the job, we kill education.

The word education is Latin and it means to lead out from darkness. The word says nothing about job preparation. Training is the word that best applies to job preparation and it is different from education. The argument can be made that in this country we have turned most education into training and have, therefore, lost the meaning of education. You may have encountered this already through conversation. When the student says what discipline he or she is studying, the first question asked is usually: What are you going to do with that? This is always the wrong question and maybe the question is an example of an inauthentic question. Maybe the questioner wants to say: That is a foolish subject to study, but instead asks the more polite question. My understanding has always been that education is something to be pursued for its own sake. Education has its own intrinsic value. I also believe that if you truly have been educated, you will find a way to be gainfully employed. If you have truly been brought out of darkness, you will learn how to learn and you will learn how to think. If you have learned these things, you will learn how to find work. Finding work is the byproduct of having received an education. Do you get the difference? It is very difficult for the student to not feed the fear but instead study what one wants because one loves it. It is a ridiculous question to ask the student what they are going to do with his/her degree? How do you know what you are going to do with something when you do not even understand what that something is yet?

This discussion of education versus training brings us to a key element in this text: process versus product. When we look at something or someone at a product, it implies seeing the thing or the person as a means to an end. When we understand process, we begin to engage with something or someone for its own sake. We let go of outcomes. Everything can be thought about within this context of process versus product. Have you ever needed to read an assignment and you count out the number of pages you need to read only to get there without comprehension of what you read? Have you ever focused on the clock and wishing for a class to end only to find that the minutes dragged and you heard nothing of the lecture? Have you ever seen a person do a job he/ she dislikes and heard them say that they will put in their time until they can retire? Have you ever seen parents push children to acquire academic skills that the child may not be developmentally ready to take on? These are all examples of stressing the product over the process. I will provide an example from my life.

When I was in graduate school and I was preparing for my comprehensive exam (the comprehensive exam is an exam covering all that you learned in your graduate program), I devoted the summer to study for the exam. When I started to study, I learned that I really did not know much about my discipline. I started to dismantle all that I learned and tried to rebuild it by truly understanding where ideas belonged. I did well on the exam but afterwards, I understood that the point of the exam was the dismantling. It wasn't so much how the applicant performed on the day of the exam. If the applicant did the tearing down and rebuilding, she or he would probably do well on the exam itself. Some of my peers in graduate school saw the exam as just another hoop to jump through before getting the Ph.D. Those people most likely failed the exam. The other thing that is very important about process is that I only understood the point of the exam after I went through the process. In other words, this is meaning that is created in retrospect.

This understanding of process versus product may sound counterintuitive because the perspective offers that the more I focus on something, the greater chance I have of missing it. The immediate application one thinks of is goals. We are all trained to have goals. Right? Well, this perspective states that focusing exclusively on the goal may be the reason we do not reach it. For instance, focusing on getting an A in class is not a good focus. Focusing instead on learning something and putting your best effort into every class everyday, puts you in a better position to earn an A. The grade, then, is not the focus but the byproduct.

Viktor E. Frankl, in his book *Man's Search for Meaning,* talks about success and happiness which has application to the concepts of process versus product. First let's look at his words on success:

> Don't aim at success-the more you aim at it and make it a target, the more you are going to miss it. For success, like happiness, cannot be pursued; it must ensue, and it only does so as the unintended side-effect of one's personal dedication to a cause greater than oneself or as the by-product of one's surrender to a person other than oneself. Happiness must happen, and the same holds for success; you have to let it happen by not caring about it.[1]

Here, sometimes students interpret Frankl's words to mean slacking off. This is not what he means. He states that you need to dedicate yourself. Dedicate is a great word. It comes from the Latin *dedicare* meaning to give out tidings (as to a religious institution) or to proclaim. There is nothing lackadaisical about Frankl's description of the work involved.

When I was teaching this concept, one very astute student noticed something about Frankl's language. She focused on the word

---

[1] Viktor Frankl, *Man's Search for Meaning* (New York: Simon & Schuster, 1959), 16-17.

"at" in the quote and observed that at means toward or because of. She noted that Frankl does not say to not aim **for** success. I think she is right. Aiming at success means a singular focus. You can receive the A in class but maybe you did not learn anything. Here, I think Frankl is stating the opposite of that which has been drilled into us and I think that it takes time to adjust to this new idea. Here are some of the things that are wrong with focusing on a product:

- Sometimes we do not know the meaning of something until it is over. (This is the retrospect I talked about earlier in graduate school.)
- Sometimes we miss things that come into our life that are far greater than that which we are aiming at and we miss them because they fall outside of our target.
- Sometimes we think we want something only to receive it and discover that is not at all what we wanted.
- Sometimes we become so focused on a particular goal that it leaves other parts of ourselves underdeveloped.
- Sometimes the aiming at success is empty and takes away any intrinsic meaning to be discovered.

This is a mindset that you have been indoctrinated in probably since you began school. The purpose usually of 1st grade is getting into 2nd grade; the purpose of high school is getting into college; the purpose of college is to get the job. This mentality never allows the student to construct meaning where she/he is. The student's eyes are frequently directed away from what she/he is currently doing. This consistent misfocus wears away at meaning. Is it any wonder that many students see school as a series of hoops to jump through and that these hoops have no intrinsic worth? This, I think, is the system that we have created and we cannot blame students who become disinterested. Having said that, it is still your responsibility to learn and make school work for you even if it is not presented in the best light.

This idea of process versus product sounds paradoxical. A paradox is a seemingly contradictory statement. The word comes from the Greek meaning beyond opinion. Here, the etymology of this word really helps because we have to go beyond opinion or beyond how things are usually presented to us to arrive at a different understanding. People who tell us to focus on goals are well-intentioned but I think they are wrong-headed.

Frankl talks about the concept of paradox within the context of psychology but we can easily make the connection to our discussion of education and school. Frankl talks about how the paradoxical intention works in a twofold way: "fear brings about that which one is afraid of, and that hyper-intention makes impossible what one wishes."[2] The way in which we have been trained can make us fail (that which we are most afraid of) and our exclusive focus on the end makes reaching it impossible. I think that many of us have experienced this scenario but attributed the failure to some character flaw in us instead of looking at our approach. Later on in the book, I will talk about how your approach is your response meaning that the way you approach someone or something is what you get back. For instance, approach someone with nastiness and that is usually what you get in return. The same applies here: our failure may not be in our character flaw but instead may be attributed to incorrect approach.

I think that it is worthwhile to return again to Frankl and listen to what he has to say about happiness:

> How well Kierkegaard expressed this in his maxim that the door to happiness opens outward. Anyone who tries to push this door open causes it to close still more. The man who is desperately anxious to be happy thereby cuts off his own path to happiness. Thus it is the end of all striving for happiness-for the supposed "ultimate" in life-proves to be in itself impossible.[3]

Along with our approach, we need to change our language. We talk about **getting** an education when we should speak about **receiving** an education. I would rather that we speak about education as a pilgrimage because that word stresses that it is a journey and the journey is the point. Being on a pilgrimage also means that you open yourself up to receiving. It is not something

---

[2] Frankl, *Man's Search for Meaning*, 147.
[3] Viktor E. Frankl, *The Doctor and the Soul* (New York: Vintage Books, 1986), 40.

that you "get" nor is it something that is due you. It requires a certain mindset and without it, you cannot enter. I know that some people will say that this idea sounds undemocratic. I think that some of our ideas about school have destroyed school. I think that school can be an amazing place where transformation occurs. This is what I am interested in restoring. When I speak about students as pilgrims, it reminds me of a trip to Cyprus. I was in a Greek Orthodox Church and I was in a long line of people walking past icons or religious pictures. The priest pulled me off the line and told me that the icons were for pilgrims. He told me that I needed to leave. He did this because I was not showing reverence toward the icon and kissing the icons like everyone else was. I did not like what he did at the time but now looking back, I see that he was right. If I wanted to be there, I would need to present myself in a way that was expected of me. Imagine if we did this in school from the time we are very small. You would need to show the proper respect in order to stay in school. To show yourself as worthy of receiving an education, you would need to do more than show up.

Education leads us out of our own idiocy. The word idiot comes from the Greek and means one's own. It is important to state that I would not use this word to describe someone who has intellectual disabilities. When I say that someone is being an idiot, I mean someone who has a choice to see things from multiple perspectives and chooses instead to see only from one's own point of view. School provides us with multiple ways of seeing. I think that the more ideas you can generate on how to see something, the more free you are. The idiot is the person who wears blinders and refuses to see through a different lens. We all are idiots from time-to-time and usually it takes conversation with others to show us this part of ourselves.

One word that I would like to see omitted from all talks about school is that of the consumer. A few years ago, the language shifted from speaking about the student to speaking about the consumer. It was a subtle and awful shift. If you are a consumer, you are buying something and I, as the teacher, am selling something. As the saying goes, the consumer is always right. It makes the student feel entitled. I see families shopping for colleges for their child and it does seem to me like they are shopping for a car. This perspective, in my opinion, has not served us. On the other hand, it is very difficult within our culture to speak of language other than the language of economics and the marketplace. That is why I introduced the language of pilgrimage. We are economic beings to be sure but we are so much more. Reducing everything to economics reduces us. One day in class, I took on the topic of the student as consumer. I asked my students: "If you were not consumers, what would you be?" They answered: producers or investors. They could not step out of the economic paradigm. They just could not see themselves any other way but in economic terms. Part of this is because of the example I gave them. The word consumer establishes an economic context and few people think outside of the established context. They are not aware that this is happening but it is. The person who speaks establishes the context and almost reflexively, the listener takes on that context. The other reason, however, is the predominance of the marketplace in our minds and in our lives. None of my students, for instance, said that if they were not consumers they could be citizens. We don't speak like this any longer although for the ancient Greeks and the classical Romans, this was the purpose of education: to produce citizens. In our culture, citizenship does not mean much to us; it seems mostly to have meaning for those trying to become American citizens. The liberal arts were founded with the intention to produce a well-rounded citizen. Now, my students who are studying the liberal arts declare it apologetically. The apology is offered by the use of the word "just" as in: "I am just studying liberal arts." The word "just" says it all.

The last shift in our language that I would like to see concerns the word job. We see school as a stopping place on our way to the ultimate pay off—the job. I have already spoken about how Frankl's language makes clear that this is not going to pan out for us. The goal that we are seeking will never come. I frequently encounter students who are studying subjects that make no sense for them: the education student who says she wants to teach but hates school, the accounting student who is not good with numbers, or the student who fancies herself becoming a doctor but is not strong in science. The examples are more common than one would think. I think that the educational system is to blame for this extreme disconnect between one's talents and abilities and one's so–called goals.

Instead of speaking about jobs, I ask my students to think about what they imagine their work to be. The word work is Latin and it means *opus* or something grand you produce with your life. As a student, part of your work is to discover what you were made to do. This discovery process always begins with an inventory of self: passions, talents, abilities, callings, etc.. Work, Frankl tells us, is one of the central ways that we create meaning in our lives. Is it any wonder so many people are miserable doing jobs they find meaningless? According to Frankl, ". . . we can discover meaning in life in three different ways: (1) by creating a work or doing a deed; (2) by experiencing something or encountering someone; and (3) by the attitude we take toward avoidable suffering."[4]

Oftentimes, my students tell me that they believe in survival of the fittest. I then point out to them that advancing Darwinism really does not work in their favor. In many people's systems, students attending a community college are not the best nor the brightest. When they speak the language of Darwin, they are actually promoting a system that advocates their demise. I would have to say that the same is true of my story and that is why I do not use the language of Darwin. I attended City College in New York during a phase of open admissions. I was not the best student in high school and if there were not open admissions, I probably would not have gotten into college. In college, I was able to turn myself around academically and I now hold a Ph.D. I don't know if Darwin would have said that I deserved that chance if he saw my S.A.T. scores.

Along with the language of social Darinism, my students frequently say things like "it is a rat race out there," or "it is a dog eat dog world," or "it is a world where you eat or are eaten." What the students do not understand is that these words are not describing a world "out there." These words create this world for both the listener and the speaker. When discussion comes down to how uncivil we seem to be with each other, maybe some of it could be traced to this language. The metaphor here suggests that both the speaker and the other are animals. Remember, figures of speech are also figures of thought.

---

[4] Frankl, *Man's Search for Meaning*, 133.

We become what we behold. We shape our tools and then our tools shape us.

Marshall McLuhan

Chapter III

Oral Culture, Written Culture and Visual Culture

In the previous chapter, I ended with some common expressions from my students. Some would say: they are just words. We live in a time when we do not seem to value the spoken word as much as we did in the past. So we need to return to the past for a different understanding of the spoken word. Earlier, I spoke about Socrates and how much he valued the spoken word. The ancient Greeks were experimenting with an emerging technology during Socrates time and that technology was the written word.

The word technology comes from the Greek *techne'* and it means art or craft. The written word, as a new technology changed us. This may be connected to the expression that we create our inventions and then our inventions create us. Our brains began to operate differently when we started to read. A similar argument is being made about television. The Academy of Pediatrics advises that children under the age of three not watch television. It is not the content that is of concern but instead the activity of watching that changes the configuration of the brain. Babies' brains are highly plastic meaning the brain can easily adapt to external stimulation.

In an oral culture, memory is key because everything that is important to the culture is handed down from generation-to-generation orally. The stories of *The Iliad* and *The Odyssey* were first oral tales before they were written down by Homer. In memorizing the story, the ancient Greek would learn moral lessons as well as pragmatic lessons. The ancient Greek would learn who and what is virtuous as well as how to tie an array of nautical knots. This ability, to remember, is what Socrates feared would

We need to recall the angel aspect of the word,
recognizing the words as independent carriers of soul
between people.

James Hillman

Chapter IV

A Choice of Words is a Choice of Worlds

A cliché is a well-worn expression. The problem is that we do not think about the expression. We just repeat it without thinking and this is the heart of the problem. We have become detached from our words. The shift that I am asking for is that we become more mindful of our words, work to regain their power, and think about what our words are doing.

I thought that I would start this section with an expression which most of us learned as children. The expression qualifies as a cliché. Most of us learned the expression: Sticks and stones may break my bones but words will never hurt me. Well-meaning parents tell this to a child after a hurtful word has been spoken and the child is feeling injured. I ask that you think about what the words are doing? What function do they provide? When you stop and think, the words do not offer the child help in that moment and the expression may create harm. Remember the guideline: does your communication hurt or help? This expression, when broken down does not help for the following reasons: 1) The response does not acknowledge the hurt of the child. The parent is saying that there is no reason to feel hurt. 2) The response does not tell the truth. Words sometimes hurt more than physical injury. I could also argue that the use of this expression could erode trust between parent and child because the parent is obviously not speaking the truth. 3) The parent is not teaching the child any strategies that are needed in dealing with the hurtful things that will inevitably come in life. 4) The parent is in fact giving tacit endorsement for using hurtful words. If you tell a child that words are unimportant, you are saying that she/he could use hurtful words towards another.

The use of this expression represents where we are with respect to language. If we understood the power of words, we would never repeat this cliché. In this book, I will continually say that words are not in opposition to action but in fact are a form of action. We live in a culture that has diminished the power of words. I would say that oppressive language does more than represent violence. Oppressive words are forms of violence.

We say that words are symbols and symbols are defined as something that represents something else. When we go into the etymology of the word symbol, a different understanding emerges. The etymology of the word symbol refers to a token that is broken in two. One part of the token is given to the host and one part of the token is given to the guest. In the future, should they come together again, they can rejoin the two parts and remember the hospitality they once shared. The story told through the etymology tells us that language is something that we share and each person involved in the communication transaction supplies a part to reconstruct the whole.

The story tells us that two people engaged in conversation assume the reciprocal roles of host and guest—giving and receiving. The etymology provides us with an understanding of a way of being in the world through the word. The psychologist James Hillman speaks of words as emissaries or beings. The philosopher Martin Heidegger speaks, too, of words as beings. It is through words, and their etymologies, that we can access a former way of being in the world. Most of our words in English come from Greek or Latin. Heidegger states that words are crusted over from too much mindless use but they lay waiting to be revealed.

Heidegger referred to the Greek word logos to convey his understanding of words. Sometimes foreign words cannot be translated with one word in English. The meaning is far more complex. The Greek word logos means the word but also everything behind the word: the meaning, the history, the idea, the intention, the breath, etc.. All of this cannot be conveyed by the English "word." The word, logos, more accurately represents how I wish to talk about language.

The title of this chapter speaks to the creative power of words. When we speak, we are not describing a world but instead creating a world through our words. This creation is always a matter of choice. We can speak about events and experiences in a multitude of ways and our words are our choice of the world we wish to create for our listeners and ourselves. For instance, let's look at a passage from Frankl's *Man's Search for Meaning*:

> It had been a bad day. On parade, an announcement had been made about the many actions that would, from then on, be regarded as sabotage and therefore punishable by immediate death by hanging. Among these were the crimes such as cutting small strips from our old blankets (in order to improvise ankle supports) and very minor "theft." A few days previously a semi-starved prisoner had broken into the potato store to steal a few pounds of potatoes. The theft had been discovered and some prisoners had recognized the "burglar." When the camp authorities heard about it they ordered that the guilty man be given up to them or the whole camp would starve for a day. Naturally, the 2,500 men preferred to fast.[6]

Frankl makes a very important shift in this passage with his language and it is a good example of the shift I am trying to explain. The condition that Frankl is talking about is the scarcity of food. The condition does not change but the language that is used can vary significantly. Here, Frankl shifts from starving to fasting and the shift is significant. If you are starving, it is more likely that you are hungry and you are being deprived of food. Fasting, on the other hand, is not taking food and it implies the element of choice. Fasting is also usually done for a higher purpose; fasting is usually done during times of religious observance where you limit your intake as an offering. Here, Frankl gives the element of choice back to men even within this very restrictive environment. His words also suggest for the reader that if the men can reach

---

[6] Frankl, *Man's Search for Meaning*, 102.

for the higher purpose of solidarity within a concentration camp, what might we be able to accomplish within our own lives?

He uses the word "naturally" as if to suggest that humans are naturally good and will choose the right thing. He also places the words theft and burglar in quotation marks to suggest that if a man steals because he is starving, can that really be considered a theft?

In class, I speak about the difference between a reaction and a response. A reaction is when one is not thinking and speaks automatically. A response is when the speaker stops and thinks about the words she/he will speak. The word respond means to promise in return, to answer. I encourage my students to think about what world they wish to create through their words and choose their words accordingly. The words we speak determine where our listeners live but they also determine where we live. Much of the damage that is done by our use of language is not necessarily because we mean to do harm; more harm is done from people not thinking.

Frankl uses the word logos to create his theory within *Man's Search for Meaning*. His use of the word logos is, though, slightly different from how I am using the word. Frankl states that the word logos means meaning and it does. It is just that meaning is one understanding of the word logos. Within his book, he develops a theory of logotherapy to describe his brand of psychotherapy centering on meaning. The author Diane Glancy states that we take words, ideas, theories, and breathe into them new life. I have taken Frankl's theory of logotherapy and changed it into logostherapy. By logostherapy, I mean a way of understanding communication as a focusing on the logos. Remember logos means the word and everything behind the word (not just the meaning). The word therapy is Greek and it comes from *therapeia* and it means to be an attendant or one who is present. Then, if we become students of logostherapy we become attendants to the word. This is a significant shift from the social scientific study of communication. Within this context, the word is everything.

Frankl demonstrates that he, too, holds the word up to the highest degree but he also at times falls into the common trap of speaking in a way that sets up the false idea that words and actions are two different things and that actions are superior to words. Frankl falls within this trap twice in *Man's Search for Meaning*.

22

> We needed to stop asking about the meaning of life,
> and instead to think of ourselves as those who were be-
> ing questioned by life—daily and hourly. Our answers
> must consist, not in talk and meditation, but in right
> action and right conduct.[7]

Again, in the same book Frankl downplays the role of words
later: "The immediate influence of behavior is always more effective than that of words."[8] I do not understand why he would
downplay words when throughout the entire book, he is using his
words to try to shift our understanding.

Most words are not neutral. Each word that we use has a negative, positive, or sometimes neutral charge. In class, I use an example offered by the former Secretary of State Madeline Albright. I
was watching the news one evening on television and the reporter
was telling of Albright's address to students at Ohio University.
We were not shown the speech and were only given Albright's account of the students. She referred to the students as "hecklers."
She used this word because she seemed to wish to create a particular world through the word. I ask my students a series of questions
about the profile of a heckler and the following picture emerges:
a young male who is probably drunk in a comedy club. One does
not usually find hecklers within college classrooms. Some students
did not even know what a heckler was exactly but they still knew
it was not positive. Albright's use of the word suggests that the
students were not to be taken seriously. The word does that very
economically. I asked the students, what word could she have used
instead of the word "heckler?" The students offered equally negative words like "disrespectful" and "immature." This speaks to
how difficult it is to create an alternate interpretation of reality to
the current one offered. No student, for instance, offers the more
positive words of dissenter or protestor. They also do not offer
the more neutral term of "people who disagree." They accept that
Albright's language describes a reality instead of creating a reality.
This is analogous to the earlier example that I offered the students: if you were not a consumer, what would you be? The word

---

[7] Frankl, 98.
[8] Frankl, 101

"consumer" creates the context of economics and it is difficult to think outside the confined box that the word has created.

We typically think of language in opposition to action. Here, I am stressing that speaking is a form of action. The question that I would like for you to think about is: what are my words doing? Oftentimes, we take our words for granted and do not think about what they are doing. If you call a child "stupid," for instance, you are creating the possibility for that child to see himself/herself as stupid. You can say to someone, or say to yourself, that what you did was stupid but that does not make you stupid. People can change what they do; it is not as easy to change what you are. When you call someone stupid, you are defining her/him as stupid.

My goal, remember, is to shift us away from speaking automatically. The goal is to think before you speak because as you have learned, once something is said it can never be taken back. I want you to ask yourself a series of questions and the more you practice this, the quicker it gets. This process is akin to learning in general. At first, it feels clumsy and awkward but after some time it feels more natural. The questions to ask are: what am I creating for myself and the person I am speaking to? Is what I am about to say helping or hurting? What are the ranges of my choices in this given moment? Sometimes we say stupid things because we are not really aware of what we are doing. We are not being thoughtful—literally, we are not thinking and second, we are not speaking with consideration for the other. For example, one day a student told how his little sister was complaining about all the work she had in sixth grade. He told her: "Just wait until you get to college. The work you have now is nothing in comparison." We then talked about what his words did for her and for him. Let's first look at him. His words did nothing to build the relationship with his sister. In fact, he did not acknowledge her and was not supportive of her in that moment. The bottom line is that, through his words, he was competing with his little sister. Why did he feel the need to do that? This happens with us sometimes. We want to be the most miserable, overworked person in the room. Sometimes, people even compete to see who really is the most miserable? This is where complaining takes you. Then if we look at the transaction through the eyes of the little sister, her brother's words are frightening. The words are not encouraging and suggest if you are struggling now, you will never make it. His words are hurtful instead of helpful. A choice of words is always a choice of worlds.

The brother could have said anything in that moment and he did not do a good job of thinking about his choices. In addition, after speaking about this as an example in class, he also realized that his words did not match his intention. He wanted to be more helpful to his sister. He just was not thinking.

My student could have helped his sister to see her experience differently by outlining options for her. I think that this is one of the greatest services we can do for each other. Sometimes, we are too close to the forest to see the trees. Other peoples' words serve to remind us that we are free—that we have options. What are the sister's options in this moment? How could the brother help? She could see that she is given too much work and is overwhelmed. She could see that she is challenged by the work because she is pushing herself and she is moving out of her comfort zone. She could see that she is given a lot of work because others see her as capable and then maybe she can see herself as capable too. Do you see how many options there are? Once someone has helped you to generate ideas about how to see an experience and has given you different language for speaking about the experience, they have given you a gift.

We frequently say that language is subjective and what that means is the speaker speaks from her/his own point of view and the listener listens from her/his point of view as well. Typically the word subjective means immersed in one's point of view while objective means an attempt to remove point of view. The important thing to understand is that we can never get beyond our own point of view although we can make an attempt at it. We say that the newspaper is objective but it really is not because there are so many choices that get made in putting out a story that it cannot be objective. For instance, some stories are noteworthy and receive coverage and some stories are not and do not receive coverage. Placement of a story also is a choice and that choice carries a consequence. Stories that are told on page one are more important than stories told on page twenty. The reporter chooses whom to speak to and how to present the story. Each choice creates consequence. The editor chooses what to cut out and what to leave in.

I sometimes say that when you are listening, you not only need to listen to what is said but you also need to listen to what is left out.

As long as you have people involved, there will be subjectivity. Science is sometimes seen as objective but it is not. Science consists of people choosing to do particular research and institutions/corporations who are funding that research. Every step along the way there are choices to be made and once the research is complete, the way in which that research is reported out is also a choice.

In medical science, for instance, there is the idea of the plasticity of the brain. This idea states that the brain is plastic and can be molded. There have been studies of people who have had traumatic brain injury or have lost function in a particular part of the brain, who can still perform the function formerly governed by the missing or injured part of the brain. Other parts of the brain can take over the function of the missing or injured part. Doctors have just recently agreed in the truth of plasticity. Doctors have been saying this is true for some time but they could not get their articles published because it went against conventional wisdom.[9] A very long time ago the German philosopher Arthur Schopenhauer said: "All truth passes through three stages. First, it is ridiculed. Second, it is violently opposed. Third, it is accepted as being self-evident."

I think that at this point, we fully understand that history is subjective. In the past I think that history textbook writers thought that they were writing objective fact when they referred to the American Indians as "savages." Of course, they used that word because the word justified how badly we treated them. We also used the word to juxtapose them to us: the civilized ones. So much of what we do with language when we encounter the other is that we demean them, put them down, and make them less than "us." As many school-children learn, different is usually never equal or better. We still see this with people who are different because of ethnicity, disability, religion, or gender orientation. We construct the other as separate from us, different from us, less than us through our language and our language justifies how we treat them. We use the word nigger, retard, or gay to put someone

---

[9] See Norman Doidge's, *The Brain That Changes Itself* (New York: Viking Press, 2007), 19.

someone or something down. These labels have never been asso-ciated with something good. Now, some people try to take these labels back and appropriate them with different meaning. I think that the use of the label is a way of destroying a person, but in a twisted way, the person is responsible for one's own destruction. I think the same position holds for the word "bitch." I encour-age my female students to never refer to themselves or any other female as a bitch. I think that the use of these destructive words are ways to get a culture to implode. If you use a negative label to refer to yourself or someone else, you are giving tacit permission for others to use that label against you.

Having said that objectivity is near impossible, I still want to say that it is something to strive toward. I have always been drawn to the philosopher Hans-Georg Gadamer's way of discussing ob-jectivity: "We have seen that the goal of all communication and understanding is agreement concerning the object."[10] We can at-tempt to strive toward objectivity when we listen to others and learn to see a bit through their eyes and we try to come to some agreement of the truth of whatever is being discussed. It is through trying to be objective in conversation that we become greater than what we would be if we only had our own points of view.

---

[10] Hans-Georg Gadamer, *Truth and Method* (New York: Crossroad Publishing, 1975), 260.

Between stimulus and response there is a space. In that space lies our freedom to choose our response. In our response lies our growth and freedom.

Viktor E. Frankl

Chapter V
Meaning and Choice

Much of this book hinges on the idea of choice. This course teaches the student to understand how everything is really the individual's choice. We speak, sometimes, in ways where we try to deny that choice because the thought itself can be overwhelming. For instance, sometimes students say that they have no choice but to come to college. They say that their parents tell them to either attend college or move out. Or the students say that the job market "forces" them to come to college. I think that we speak this way because it is easier to think that I am being forced to do something instead of feeling the weight of one's own decisions and choices. We also think that we are doing what others want us to do because, if things do not work out, we have a scapegoat and someone or something to blame.

The truth is that there is no escape from personal responsibility. Everything I do is my choice. This is one of the privileges or downfalls (depending on your point of view) to being an adult. Children are not responsible. Children live their lives by having others direct them. Once you are an adult, all of that changes. If you are now in college, it is because you choose to be in college and making that choice brings with it certain responsibilities. When we speak of ourselves as victims or as being obedient, we do not carry the same amount of moral obligation. This, I think, is why many people act irresponsibly. I had a student once from Haiti who told me that he would never miss a class because once he registered, he saw that he entered into a contract. When I speak about this student in the classroom, I always say that it is clear that this student is not an American. We typically do not speak nor think this way.

When students state that they are being forced to come to college, they are speaking in a way that negates their own free will. They are also speaking a lie. You are being forced when someone puts a gun to your head—that is when you have no choice but to comply. In this circumstance, your choice is being taken away. Everything else is a choice.

Frankl's entire theory hinges on meaning and choice. Frankl states that between stimulus and response there is a space. In that space lies our freedom to choose our response. In our response lies our freedom. With our freedom always comes responsibilities. I think that my Haitian student may understand this concept a whole lot better than my American students. We, as a culture, tend to speak about our rights but rarely do we have a national conversation about our responsibilities.

I take the choice of words as my starting place. I invite my students to wonder about what words mean and I encourage them to think about the communicative choices they make every single moment of every single day. The choice to say or do nothing is still a choice and it (like all choices) has consequences. As soon as we begin to speak about choice, we are immediately led into the realm of consequence. I encourage my students to think about the consequences of their words before they speak them—i.e. to formulate a response instead of a reaction. Frankl calls this the categorical imperative: "Live your life as if you were living already for the second time and as if you had acted the first time as wrongly as you are about to act now!"[11]

Frankl also tells us that we as modern day people are lost. We have cut ourselves off from most of the traditions that people used to anchor their lives and give their lives meaning. He refers to this condition as the existential vacuum and describes it like this:

> No instinct tells him what he has to do, and no tradition tells him what he ought to do; sometimes he does not even know what we wishes to do. Instead, he either wishes to do what other people do (conformism) or he does what other people wish him to do (totalitarianism).[12]

---

[11] Frankl, *Man's Search for Meaning*, 133.
[12] Frankl, *Man's Search for Meaning*, 128

This quote of Frankl's is a good one to contemplate because I think that he accurately describes our current condition. When I ask students what they think they would like to do with their lives, they seem to have never thought about the question. It may seem obvious but there are many times in my life, some quite serious, where I did not realize that I did ask any questions until after the experience was over. Medical procedures that I went through come to mind. It was only after the experience that I realized my own ignorance and my own lack of awareness about my own ignorance. Sometimes we are not aware that we are not asking questions.

We find ourselves in college with no understanding of the meaning of college nor an understanding of why we are here. We are here because everyone else is (conformism) or we are here because others have told us that we need to be here (totalitarianism). This, I think, is a recipe for disaster. We can choose to live a meaningless life but it will always take a toll. I do not think that it is hyperbole to say that drug and alcohol abuse, in some part, stem from a feeling of meaninglessness. I think also that our culture does not encourage young people to create meaning. If you are always focused on where you are going next, then you are being trained to not live in the present and you are not given the opportunity to create meaning from where you are. If you come to college not knowing what you wish to study and what you wish to do, that is exactly where you are supposed to be. How can you know when you have no experience? Some people do know when they are quite young as to the path their life will take. My friend, Ellen, told her mother at the age of nine that she wanted to play piano, become a doctor, and marry Peter! And she did all those things.

Most of us figure it out as we go along. Learning about your passions, talents, and interests is a process. You cannot know if you never fully enter into the experience. This does mean that you become lackadaisical about your pursuits. You keep putting yourself in the path of discovering what you are meant to do, what you have an aptitude for, and how you can think about earning a living doing what you love. Some people create meaning retrospectively.

What I think most do not understand is that our choices create us. If you are disinterested in school, bored, and putting in very little effort that is the type of person you are creating. It is very difficult to become focused, attentive, and enthusiastic if you have been practicing living its opposite. Learning is a choice. If you choose to learn, you will. If you choose not to learn, you will not. I used to work recruiting employees for a large investment bank in New York. The traits that employers most look for are getting along with others, the ability to learn, and the ability to learn on your own. When I ask students to name the traits most employers seek, they never mention these. They do not mention these because students are not thinking enough from the other's perspective. For instance, students usually say that employers are seeking people who are ambitious. When you think about from the employer's point of view, what use does ambition play?

Employers want someone who will not be caustic in working with others. They want someone who can learn because the marketplace is always changing. They want those who can teach themselves because that saves the organization time and money on training. When you look at school from this perceptive, the **what** you are studying becomes less important than **that** you are studying, and **how** you are studying.

So this idea of choice and meaning starts to significantly shift the way we see things. Frankl states, as do many others, that we cannot change our situations. We can, though, change how we see our situations. The faculty that allows us to see things in a multitude of ways is imagination. I think this is why Einstein said that imagination is more important than knowledge. The more ideas we can generate and the more we use our imaginations, the more choices we have. The more choices we have, the more free we are. If we only see something one way, we are more restricted and less free. This restricted and narrow way of seeing life is the way of the idiot (from idios meaning one's own). Frankl states that attitude is everything and our attitude is our own choice. Frankl tells us that the men in the concentration camp were able to choose their attitudes. As we read this, we must understand that if concentration camp prisoners can do this so can we. Frankl observes:

> We who lived in concentration camps can remember the men who walked through the huts comforting others, giving away their last piece of bread. They may

have been few in number, but they offer sufficient proof that everything can be taken from a man but one thing: the last of human freedoms—to choose one's attitude in any given set of circumstances, to choose one's own way.[13]

This argument runs against the idea that we as humans are conditioned which is to say that our situations or environments create us. According to the philosophy that Frankl is attaching his thought to, existentialism, states that we create ourselves. As adults, then, we are fully responsible for our own lives—no exceptions. This, I call, radical responsibility because one can never blame another for one's own life. We are given situations in life and if we are undone by hardship, it is because we choose to see hardship as our undoing. This is tough medicine and it flies in the face of the litigious culture in which we live. If our courts were governed by an existentialist philosophy, they would look very different than they look now. The most egregious example of a lawsuit completely lacking in personal responsibility was known as the "Twinkie Defense" in the 1970's. A man was accused of murder and his lawyer argued that he was not accountable for his actions because he ate too much junk food.

This idea of personal responsibility pushes us back upon ourselves and with all these ideas, you can look at them macroscopically or microscopically. The Twinkie Defense is an example of how personal responsibility might be looked at macroscopically (in the big picture). Examples of how this idea of personal responsibility can be looked at microscopically come from within your classroom. For example, you miss class on a day an assignment is due and you come to class the next day to hand in the assignment. The student typically says: "I missed class last time so here is my paper." If you are in my class, I will hand you the paper back. The student usually does not understand. If you missed a class and missed an assignment, it is then your responsibility to live with the consequence of missing that assignment. Handing the assignment to me is presumptuous on the student's part. The assumption is that I will accept it. Something that makes the situation

---

[13] Frankl, *Man's Search for Meaning*, 86.

better is when the student at least tells me why the deadline was missed because it is a sign of respect. Something that makes the situation much worse is when the student leaves the paper on my desk without a word because that shows disrespect. Remember, how you approach someone is what you get in return. When I see a late paper on my desk, I want to throw it back on the student's desk. The best approach, if you miss a deadline, is to come to class the next day and tell your teacher why you missed the deadline. Have the paper ready to hand in and say: "I realize that this is late and I am hoping that you will still accept it. If you will not, I understand." This, in a nutshell, is the language of personal responsibility. The reason students do not do this is because they have never been asked to act responsibly.

While we are fully responsible for ourselves, we are in no position to tell others how they should live their lives or what meanings they should create. Frankl tells us that there is no such thing as a general meaning of life but all life does have meaning. It is the work of each individual to figure out what that meaning is. According to Frankl:

> These tasks, and therefore the meaning of life, differ from man to man and from moment to moment. Thus it is impossible to define the meaning of life in a general way. Questions about the meaning of life can never be answered by sweeping statements. "Life" does not mean something vague, but something very real and concrete.[14]

Sometimes, we encounter people who act as if the world owes them a living. This is the height of being irresponsible. This book stresses the understanding that life, and the world, owes us nothing. We need to shift the onus of responsibility to ourselves. Life does not come to us with meaning. We need to create meaning in our own lives. Frankl puts it this way:

> What was really needed was a fundamental change in our attitude toward life. We had to learn ourselves

---

[14] Frankl, *Man's Search for Meaning*, 98

and, furthermore, we had to teach the despairing men, that *it did not really matter what we expected from life, but rather what life expected from us.*[15]

This shift is a significant one. This is a similar shift that John F. Kennedy was speaking about when he said: "Ask not what your country can do for you. Ask what you can do for your country." This shift is a shift from self-centeredness to being responsible. Later in the book, I will speak about how it is also a shift from getting to giving. The important thing to note here is that our expectations for life really have no meaning. Life will take its own course regardless of our expectations. When we look at life this way, to have particular expectations is foolish. We feel that if we have certain expectations for life, they should come true. We think that life should conform to our expectations and when it doesn't, we may become angry. It is always us who need to conform to life, to accept what is and, as I will later show, always try to make the very best out of that which we have been given.

I stress throughout the entire book that everything starts and ends with you. Only when you attribute meaning to something does something have meaning. Entering the class, I ask that you open yourself up to creating meaning. Understand that everything has the potential for meaning and you need to become educated so that you can respond. I start the class with the students telling the story of their names. I have my own list of reasons but I use the experience as a heuristic exercise where the student is invited to discover her/his meaning. Our name is the first gift we were given. Some of us have never thought about the gift or we take the gift for granted. Some of us feel, in a chauvinistic way, if it is our name then it must be the best. Others take pride in the story of their origins and display respect towards those who named them.

There are many ways to construct meaning from the exercise of telling the story of our names. 1) Once you speak, you emerge as a person in the class. 2) When you tell the story of your name, you emerge as a person with history, who has a background and a family. 3) You tell others how you see yourself and how you see

---

[15] Frankl, *Man's Search for Meaning,* 98

us by how you speak the story. 4) Like our names, all words have stories. 5) The stories take us away from words as mere abstractions and toward something concrete in the world. 6) How can the story of one's name provide you with a way of seeing yourself? 7) Through the sharing of the stories, we replicate the oral culture of the ancient Greek or the preliterate child. 8) Oral culture relies on being present in the moment and stresses listening. 9) If one is present, you will tend to remember more. 10) What strategies can one employ to assist memory? These strategies were called mnemonics by the Greeks and were aids to memory.

For most, it is both empowering and difficult to realize that everything is our choice. In some ways, it is easier to see oneself as a victim of circumstance. Within the framework of this book, to see oneself as a victim comes down to a choice.

What we perceive and understand depends on what we are.

Aldous Huxley

Chapter VI
Perception

In the previous chapter, I talked about a way of seeing. When we speak about ways of seeing, we are in the realm of perception. Perception is key to understanding how communication works. We frequently take our perceptions for granted. We think that the way we see something is the way it is. We need instead to shift our understanding about perception. Perception is a construct. Our perceptions of the world are a reflection of our state of consciousness. This means that everything that makes up who we are (gender, education, ethnicity, age, religion, sexual orientation, abilities) shapes what we see. Our perceptions are always colored by our own experiences. In order to explicate how perception works, I will offer some examples from Frankl, then I will talk about some common tendencies that we have regarding our perceptions, and last I will offer some real-life examples so that you can have a firm grasp of the concept so that you can apply it to your life.

Frankl offers us the example of a rabbi grieving the loss of his family to the concentration camps. His grief goes deeper, however, when Frankl asks him a question regarding the rabbi's hope of seeing his children in Heaven after death:

> However, my question was followed by an outburst of tears, and now the true reason for his despair come to the fore: he explained that his children, since they died as innocent martyrs, were thus found worthy of the highest place in Heaven, but as for himself he could not expect, as an old, sinful man, to be assigned the same place. I did not give up but retorted, "Is it not

conceivable, Rabbi, that precisely this was the meaning of your surviving your children: that you may be purified through these years of suffering, so that finally you, too, though not innocent like your children, may *become* worthy of joining them in Heaven?"[16]

It is only through understanding the rabbi's religious foundation that Frankl can offer him a new perspective. The rabbi's experience went far beyond grief and he needed a different point of view on his experience and that is precisely what Frankl offered him. Frankl offered the rabbi a different way of seeing his own experience. This is where others come into our lives. Sometimes we are too close to our own experience to see it any other way but one way. Others, such as friends, families, teachers, parents, therapists, offer us other ways of seeing and can therefore change our perceptions.

Frankl tells us that suffering, once we discover its meaning, ceases to be suffering. That is to say once we have a different perception of suffering, we no longer see ourselves as suffering. The suffering, then, may be seen as a divine gift which offers us insight. This is what Frankl means when he tells us to be worthy of our suffering. He means that we should transform the suffering by gaining some insight. The opposite of this is to become a victim where we wallow in the suffering and never create meaning from it. Frankl states, "Emotion, which is suffering, ceases to be suffering as soon as we form a clear and precise picture of it."[17] Frankl tells of an elderly doctor who was suffering from severe depression. He was depressed because his wife, whom he loved dearly, had died. Again, Frankl asks a question instead of giving an answer. He asks how it would have been had the physician died first and his wife survived him. The man responded that it would have been awful because then his wife would have suffered. Frankl then concluded that his suffering is the sacrifice he is making to spare his wife.[18]

---

[16]Frankl, *Man's Search for Meaning*, 142.
[17]Frankl, *Man's Search for Meaning*, 95.
[18]Frankl, *Man's Search for Meaning*, 135.

One of the things that I like about Frankl's work is that he shows the futility of trying to change situations. We frequently act like reality should conform to us when it needs to be the other way around. Wishing, hoping and wanting reality to conform to us can be crazy making. Frankl states: "When we are no longer able to change a situation—just think of an incurable disease such as inoperable cancer—we are challenged to change ourselves."[19] This also applies to the futility of trying to change another person. The only thing we can change is how we see the other person or change ourselves.

Frankl offers examples of how reality may be perceived in many different ways depending on one's experience. For example, he offers the context of people looking at pictures taken within a concentration camp. He states that others look at the pictures in horror (which is a legitimate response) but from within the context of the camps, he can look at the people in the pictures as lucky! How can they be lucky? They are lucky because they are alive and for the moment, they are resting in cots instead of out working in horrific conditions. So, Frankl shows how even a photograph taken during one of the worst times in history, may be seen differently through different eyes.

We need to understand how we see things may not be how they are. An example of this comes from an experience with my son. I have twin boys and one of my boys has cerebral palsy. Cerebral palsy is a condition that affects motor function and as a result of cerebral palsy, my son does not yet walk, talk, or feed himself independently. One day, we took our sons for ice cream. After the first mouthful, my son started to scream. I held him because I knew it was a scream of pain but I did not know the cause at that time. Two women walked past us and said: "Another brat having a temper tantrum." My son could have been a brat having a tantrum but he wasn't. He was in pain. After that incident, I discovered that he had several cavities in his mouth and could not tolerate dairy. The cold ice cream was the perfect storm to send him over the edge.

---

[19]Frankl, *Man's Search for Meaning,* 135.

Sometimes we are told something so often that we think it is true when it is not. A case in point is the story I often tell in class of the "stolen" purse. I was in the women's bathroom in school when a woman came out of the stall and said that someone had just stolen her purse. I asked how that was true since I was standing there and saw no one. The woman said that she placed her bag on the hook inside the door and it was gone. The woman explained to me that her mother was a police officer and repeatedly told her not to place her bag there because thieves reach over and grab bags. Again, I told her that I saw no one. The next day, I saw this woman again at school and I inquired about the bag. She then told me that it was in her car the whole time. She never brought the bag into school. This is an example of how we come to believe something is true when the message is repeated to us. A good application of this idea is television. We watch a commercial, or a news item, over and over and in our minds it becomes true. Repetition of messages is very persuasive.

We can also form a perception and then make everything we experience fit within that perception. Two personal examples come to mind. One happened when I was writing my master's thesis at home. I heard a call for help outside my window. I opened the window to see a man across the courtyard calling for help in an adjacent apartment. The man said: "We are locked in the bathroom. Can you go for help?" I told him yes and started to put on my shoes but as I did, I started to wonder. I wondered if he, too, were writing his thesis and was doing research on how many people come to the aid of someone calling for help. I did not think about the odds of this being true. I kept going. I left my apartment and called for the elevator. When the elevator arrived, a man was standing there with only a pair of jeans on—no shirt and no shoes. I concluded that this man was also in on the experiment and was there to inform "the researcher" that I had left my apartment. Once we arrived in the lobby, I became suspicious. I thought maybe the man in the window wanted to get me into his building. My suspicions were piqued enough that I now knew I was not entering the building alone. I called on the superintendent of my building and told him the situation. He and I went to the superintendent of the other building and asked him to check on one of his tenants. The end result was that the man was locked in the bathroom with his girlfriend. The partially dressed man I encountered in the elevator was a worker in the building and was going to the basement to do his laundry. Everything else was my fabrication based on my own experience.

Another example comes from a friend of mine and I think that it is instructive because, like the man in the bathroom window, it speaks about how we interpret other people's comments based upon our own experience. My friend and a group of his friends rented a ski house. One woman brought her new fiancé to the house and my friend did not like him. He confided his feeling to another housemate. One day, my friend came home from work and the friend who brought the fiancé left the following message: "I spoke to Bob and I understand that you have some negatives. Can you give me a call?" My friend then immediately called Bob and accused him of breaking his confidence. Bob swore that he said nothing about the fiancé. Then, my friend wondered, how could she know that he had negative feelings toward the fiancé? He called the woman who left the message and discovered that she was talking about pictures. She wanted the negatives of the pictures! This is a case of a guilty conscious creating a perception of reality.

One day, I was attending a workshop on education and the teacher offered the following example from a math lesson. The teacher was asking a little boy to answer a question that she had written on the board. If you take away three from five, she asked pointing to numbers she had written, how many are left? The boy answered that none were left. As the teacher, you can conclude many different things from his response: he does not understand subtraction, he did not understand the question, or he cannot see the board. I do not think that most teachers' minds would consider what the boy was really responding to. To him, all the numbers were lined up and in the center. There were no numbers to the left; all the numbers were written in the middle. It takes a creative mind to consider this as a potential interpretation for the question. Kids are difficult because while they can respond, as this boy did, he probably cannot tell you why he is responding as he did. Some other examples from kids are thinking if you are in back-to-back meetings all day that you literally went through the day with a person on your back. Or if you offer them a make-up lesson, he/she will be instructed on how to put on make-up or how to make up with a person. My son, when he was three, thought that the kiddie pool was an entire pool for cats! When he was older, he thought that a help wanted sign in a retail window was really a bulletin announcing a crime because it said: Wanted. Man with van.

I use the example of two students embracing to teach how perception works. I told the students that I saw two students sitting on the bench outside the classroom kissing. I asked them what they would think if they encountered the lovers. As predicted, those students who were in happy relationships saw the couple in a positive light. Those students who were not in a relationship saw the couple as flaunting something that should be kept private. Those students, who came from restrictive cultures, saw the students as committing a sin. This exercise gets more complicated when I state that the couple was homosexual. Then, there is even a different response to being told that the couple is two men or that the couple is two women. It would be different still if I said that the couple is elderly or different skin colors. All of these examples tell us how our experience, background, and culture shapes what we see.

In communication, there is the expression that language shapes perception and perception shapes language. What something is called has a huge influence on our perceptions. A good example of this comes from food. There used to be a food product in this country called horse mackerel. No one bought it and it sat on the shelves. They pulled the product, changed the name and the label. The old product of horse mackerel sold very well as tuna fish. Food provides us lots of examples about how our culture instructs us as to what is eatable and what is not. In this country, we are loath to eat anything with horse in its name except maybe horse-radish whereas in Venice, I remember visiting a butcher shop that sold nothing but horse meat. My favorite example of how language shapes perception is the case of homework. You can write, draw, or create with a child and for most, it will be fun. Once the activity is called homework, it is no longer perceived to be something fun or worthwhile. I also think that schools create some of this negative perception by linking homework with punishment. Students, if they misbehave, are given extra homework instead of giving extra homework as a reward for being well behaved. (When

I say that last statement, students cannot even imagine homework in such a positive light.)

So we can see from this experience how language shapes perception. It may also be the reason why certain foods are given names that seem to have nothing to do with the contents. Sweetbreads, for instance, are neither sweet nor bread but rather the internal organs of an animal. We can see that perceptions also shape language. If you have a good impression or perception of school, the language that you use to talk about school will reflect your favorable perceptions. If you have a poor perception of school, it will not take long for your listener to hear that perception as well.

There are some common tendencies with regard to perception and I think it may be worthwhile to review them. There are several types and like most things, they are more complicated than you would think.

1) We make snap judgments.
2) We cling to first impressions.
3) We judge ourselves and those with whom we are in relationship with more charitably than we judge others.
4) We are influenced by our expectations.
5) We tend to ignore the obvious.
6) We assume others are like us.[20]

First, we make snap judgments. Judgments are a difficult thing to talk about because being judgmental clearly is wrong and gets us into trouble. Racism and stereotyping are examples of being judgmental and we need to bring consciousness to what we are doing when we have these perceptions. We need to interrogate them and examine where they came from. Judgment, on the other hand, is very different and we need to learn the difference. If, for instance, you do not feel safe in the company of another, you need to know whether that is being judgmental and then you need to ignore it or if you are rendering a judgment and therefore need to pay attention. I will say more about this when I speak about

---

[20] This list comes from *Interplay: The Process of Interpersonal Communication* by Adler, Rosenfeld, and Proctor (New York: Oxford University Press, 2010). I have changed we are influenced by the obvious to we ignore the obvious because I think we often look right past the obvious.

our response to others. I think, too often, we are talked out of (by ourselves or by others) our own judgments. I think that we need to be aware of our snap judgments but not wed ourselves to them.

Second, this leads to the tendency of clinging to first impressions. This is another example of how we ask reality to conform to us. If we have evidence to disregard the impression, we need to disregard it because to do otherwise is to ask that the other not be who they truly are. Our first impressions may be formed by what we already know. Again, here we are talking about how we create or manufacture a version of reality. For example, a teacher may be told that one of her students has a disability. The child's actions are then filtered through that lens. Here, how the teacher responds is determined by what disability means to this individual teacher.

Third, we judge ourselves and those with whom we are in a relationship more charitable than we judge others. We use different language when speaking about those we know as contrasted with those we do not know. There are many examples such as you or your friends are free spirits but others whom you do not know are sluts. When you are angry, your anger is justified but others are explosive or loose cannons. If you get caught cheating, you were trapped but others are unethical. Two examples from the classroom come to mind. One day, I was going over the requirements for the paper and a student slept the entire time. I let him sleep. At the end of class, he came up to ask me the requirements for the paper. I said: What makes you think I will answer your questions when you made the choice to sleep when I reviewed the requirements? The student told me that he was not sleeping. I told him that I saw him and yes, indeed, he was sleeping. Finally, the student said: "I was not sleeping, I was dozing." Oh. Another example comes from a student's writing where the student wrote: "I witnessed a robbery when a friend of mine decided to commit a mistake." His friend committed a mistake but another would have committed a crime. All of these examples offer how we frequently have a self-serving bias in our language. We speak more favorably about ourselves and our friends because we are trying to protect ourselves and those we care about. We are trying to protect ourselves from the truth about ourselves or someone we care about. We do not have such altruism toward those whom we do not know.

The example I offered previously about the child with the disability is also connected to being influenced by our expectations.

This is one tendency that we do not wish to think about because it states that what we expect, we find. This idea states that our experience is more controlled than we would like to admit. For instance, if you expect to have a good time at school, you usually do. Conversely, if you expect to be bored at school, you will be. This is another reinforcement of the idea that circumstances and situations do not create us as we think they do but rather we create us. We sometimes do not wish to admit that we have this power because with this power, comes responsibility. Imagine thinking that everything I now have in my life is the result of my own choice? It certainly does create a shift—doesn't it?

The tendency that we tend to ignore the obvious is complicated. We ignore the obvious things like a child who grows up watching too much television may have difficulty paying attention in school. The issue may not be caused by a condition such as attention deficient but rather by what the child has been fed. Diet, here, may refer to food or media. If a person is not fed properly, there will most likely be a negative consequence. Diet is my example of overlooking the obvious because it seems that we live in a time where adults are quick to turn symptoms into pathology without looking at other factors first. Another example may be that when a divorce happens, we frequently look to see who is to blame. Both are always to blame since they are in a relationship. Whatever is created is the responsibility of both parties. Even if one leaves the relationship, it is never clear to outsiders who left the relationship first.

My previous story of responding to the man locked in his bathroom can also be used as support for the tendency to assume that others are like us. I was writing my Master's thesis at the time and the first thought that I had was he was working on his own thesis to see how many people would come to his assistance. The thought did cross my mind that this was a staged experiment!

In addition to the common tendencies of perception, there are some additional features that need to be addressed. In class, I will bring in a box of objects.[21] What the objects have in common is that they are not easily recognizable. I use the objects to serve as heuristic devices for teaching some additional features of perceptions. Here is list to help guide our discussion: 1) How

---

[21] I am deeply indebted to Dr. Grace Fala at Juniata College for the use of this exercise. Grace is a masterful teacher from whom I continually learn.

45

something is presented shapes perception. 2) We are fearful about expressing ideas. 3) We are not accustomed to using our imaginations. 4) We are fearful that we may be wrong about what we think we know. 5) When something is taken out of context, it changes how we see it. 6) We typically do not ask questions. 7) What we say about the objects says more about us than about the objects. 8) We need others to point out what they see and then once we see it, it seems obvious. 9) What we do with objects, we do with people. 10) Sometimes we want to know what something is called so that we have closure. Closure is sometimes the end of thought. This is a long list so let's start unpacking it.

How something is presented usually shapes my perception of it. This is an important idea to grasp because how something is presented is usually subtle and we are not usually aware of how much we are being influenced. When I taught at Penn State, I showed my students a film called One Film: Three Scripts. It was a film about Puerto Rico. The visuals remained the same but there were three different narratives from three different points of view. One narrative was from the tourist point of view where poverty-stricken parts of the island were explained away as to not scare the tourists. The second point of view was a communist/socialist point of view and the poverty is presented as the direct result of capitalism. The last point of view advocates mainland benevolence toward the islanders. All the improvements to the island are presented as helpful interventions. I try to present a similar message with objects. For instance, most people do not see what is in actuality an ankle harness for an animal as a swing for a bird until I begin to mimic the action of a swing. I used the example of how homework is presented as if it were punishment thereby shaping the impression that it is a punishment.

Many times after I say what an object is, a student will say that she/he thought of that answer. My question is then, why didn't you say it? The answer is usually because we are afraid. What if no one sees it as I do? What if no one agrees with me? What if people laugh at me? These are the fears that stop us. It is difficult to say what you think and to do so always involves a risk. If we choose to stand, we need to take the risk to stand alone. This choice needs to be made on a case-by-case basis. It is foolish to always take a risk and it is cowardly to never take a risk. This goes back to the idea of respond versus react spoken about earlier. Some people always take risks, even when they should not, and some people never take risks, even when they should. Both are reacting instead of responding. Saying the first thing that comes to your mind is usually a reaction and it is usually speech without thought. All of us could, at some point in our lives, have felt the sting of being in the minority—the minority of public opinion. If you have never felt this, then, you are not responding nor are you speaking from an authentic point of view. You are repeating safe ideas and clichés. You then sound like everyone else and your speech really says nothing other than communicating to the world that you do not think for yourself or you are too frightened to speak what you think. The important point here is to come back around to the central idea that everything is our choice and our choices create us.

When I present the objects to my students in class, I am usually struck by how we are not accustomed to using our imaginations. I frequently ask the students to imagine this activity with little kids. Most little kids can see a lot because they live in the world of imagination. It is important to hold on to imagination not in the sense of creating fantasy but in the sense of having many images that come to mind. The more images we have, the more choices we have. The more choices we have, the freer we are. If I only see things, people, or objects one way then I am limited. If I can learn how to see through different points of view then I have more options. Also, if I can see through different points of view, I am better prepared to understand others. Difficulties between us are usually attributed to problems of sight. We do not see the other's point of view and that is a limitation within ourselves. Those disciplines that cultivate imagination, art and music, are essential for sharing the world with others. Those who advocate eliminating the arts really do not understand the role they play within our lives.

We sometimes hold firmly to what we think we know. Using my point about the arts in education as example may work here. There are those who maintain that the arts are something like a past time—not really essential. They then hold on to this idea as "the truth." People who hold this point of view may become threatened if someone comes along and challenges what is held to be true. We all maintain certain truths in our minds and these truths provide us with some kind of stability and safety. That is why you may see people become extremely defensive when these truths are challenged. In order to be in a shared public world, we need to maintain that our opinion and point of view is merely one way and there are multiple ways of seeing. Once we have learned to see differently, we may give up some of what we hold to be the truth. This takes a tremendous amount of maturity because most times, we are fearful about being wrong about what we think we know.

Much of the talk about perceptions is about being aware of what we take for granted. Context is something we usually take for granted. Context provides us with information on how to interpret a message. If you know a little bit of a foreign language, you may understand what I am speaking about. If you have a basic grasp on a foreign language but are not fluent, you can frequently understand a conversation provided that you know the context. The context is the situation surrounding the talk. For instance, if you hear someone say, "this case is heavy," it helps if you know that the speakers are lawyers or movers. Context, like many of these ideas, is a very important idea to understand for media literacy. A message taken out of context changes how the message is interpreted. There are many examples of politicians who have said a message and then on the evening news, that message is taken out of its original context. The end result is a very different message.

Context is always very important in communication because what is appropriate within one context is not appropriate within another. In communication, this concept is known as rhetorical sensitivity. Rhetorical sensitivity is the speaker's ability to adapt to different situations. For instance, you cannot address me in the classroom as you would your friend. If you speak to everyone the same way, it shows a lack of rhetorical sensitivity. I had a student in my class once who boasted that he spoke to everyone the same way. He saw this as a sign of democracy and fairness. This same student frequently blurted out comments that made his classmates roll their eyes. I thought that this is sometimes where a person's idea of egalitarianism leads. This student needed to learn to speak to us differently than how he spoke to his family or friends. I am not saying that we all need to become phony. What we need is a repertoire of ways of speaking much the same way as a musician needs a repertoire of songs. If you only know how to play one song, you are limited. The more songs you can play, the more audiences for which you can play.

I sometimes show a film clip of the chairman of Union Carbine—the company responsible for the environmental disaster at Love Canal. I show two film clips. One clip shows Mr. Kennedy speaking to stockholders at a cocktail party. He tells a folksy story of how his dog bit his mailman. The moral of the story, as Mr. Kennedy explains it, is that one cannot give away one's problems. The story went over just fine for the first audience. The next clip shows Mr. Kennedy delivering the same speech at a town hall meeting. The audience explodes and Mr. Kennedy looks shocked. One man in the audience rises up to say: "Our children are sick and you are telling us a story about your dog!" Mr. Kennedy, you would think, would have advisers to inform him that speaking about a petty example in the context of environmental disaster is to belittle and insult the audience. It is adding harm to a preexisting condition.

It may have been better had Mr. Kennedy began by asking questions instead of making statements. The longer I teach, the more I see how we do not ask questions. I frequently tell my students that I wish teachers would reward the intelligent questions instead of rewarding the correct answer. I speak about developing a sense of wonder. The mind, in a place of wonder, does not make statements but asks questions. Here, again, is where little kids are superior. Little kids ask wonder-full questions because of how they see the world. The mind that thinks it knows it all does not ask wonder-full questions. When I show the objects, I am struck by how few questions I receive. Infrequently does someone say: what is it made out of, where does it come from, or what is it used for? The best questions are usually: may I see the object closer, or may I hold the object? We have been trained not to ask these kinds of questions whereas they usually are the first questions little kids will ask. Sometimes we are not even aware that we are not asking questions. I have been in situations myself where it was only clear in retrospect how I did not ask any questions. I have written a book on medical communication where I discuss the questions I did not ask.[22]

---

[22] See my What Do the Doctors Say?: How Doctors Create a World Through Their Words (Bloomington, IN: iUniverse, 2010). In this book, I apply the idea of how words create worlds to the medical community.

Sometimes we do not ask questions because we are fearful of appearing stupid. A student once told me that she will never ask another question in school because when she was in the sixth grade, she asked what language the people in China spoke? She never lived that question down. I told her that silencing herself is not a wise choice having asked one foolish question. Asking questions can also be a way to not make oneself appear foolish. I use myself as an example in the classroom to illustrate how stupid it sometimes is to make pronouncements instead of wisely asking questions. I was in an academic meeting at school with all the members of my department. We were asked to read a course description about one of our courses and comment upon it. The description was very one-dimensional and, in my opinion, did not fully represent the entire course. I said, "The person who wrote this statement clearly doesn't understand our discipline." It was then that the chair of the department, who came from outside the disciple, said: "I wrote it." I wanted to crawl under the chair. If I had asked: I wonder who wrote this? Instead, I made a pronouncement and I ended up looking foolish. I still hold by the opinion that the statement did not represent the course fully but if I had known that the writer was present, I could have presented the message differently. My words were stupid because I did not think before I spoke.

I tell my students that our messages, even when we are speaking about others, always reveal ourselves. In the example cited above, in that moment during the meeting I revealed that I was not thinking about what I was saying. Even though I thought I was speaking about the writer, I was speaking about myself. If we return to the objects, sometimes I have a student present who says that every object I show is a weapon. Every object could be a weapon if I see it as a weapon. Also every object could be a piece of art and a thing of beauty if I see it that way. One time while I was showing the objects in class, a student said that all the objects were junk and if he came across them he would throw them in the trash. The objects, I need to say, are precious to me and hold special meaning. Each object, for me, holds a story and contains memory of experience and relationship. My student's comment about them being trash tells me more about him than it tells me about the objects. His comment tells me that I could never trust him because he does not know how to honor another's experience. He seems to be of the belief that if the object has no meaning for him, it holds no meaning. If I were in a relationship with this young man, I would never show myself to him because he, through his words, showed me that he was not to be trusted.

Most times, though, we can learn from listening to others. I may not see something as significant but I can learn to see it that way through another's eyes. This is the way we become greater, bigger, and more than what we are alone. This is why we need each other interpersonally. Other people can teach me how to see by describing what it is they see. Many of us have seen the picture used to teach this aspect of perception. It is the picture of a woman: look at the picture one way and you see a younger woman. Look at the picture another way and you see an older woman. People usually see it one way. Those who see the younger woman can learn to see the older woman and vice versa. To take this to the next level, you can try to see both the older woman and the younger woman simultaneously. Those who can accomplish both visions simultaneously have a better chance of holding two opposing ideas in their heads at the same time. The writer F. Scott Fitzgerald said that this was the sign of a first-rate mind. If you can hold two opposing points in your head at the same time, you can follow someone's line of reasoning without forgetting your own. Some people claim that they need to interrupt because if they do not, they will forget what they wanted to say. This, then, is just announcing how feeble-minded they are.

What I find so interesting about how the human mind works is that once we see something or know something, it then seems obvious. We do not seem to recall that we always did not see it this way. We may also become impatient with learners who are trying to learn what we have learnt. We very rarely are empathetic toward the learner. Just think about trying to teach your little brother how to tie his shoe or giving your mother directions. I think about the truth of the words of the philosopher Schopenhauer: All truth passes through three stages. First, it is ridiculed. Second, it is violently opposed. Third, it is accepted as self-evident. We frequently do not remember the process that we went through to get where we are. It seems like we always knew and that is why we are so impatient with those who are in the process of learning.

The objects are a simple representation for very complicated ideas. I want us to also reflect on the fact that what we do with objects, we also do with people. We frequently do not take the time to experience another being. We are not fully paying attention. The objects, like other people, are unknown and the experience is meant to serve as a heuristic for how we experience the unknown. Some people ignore the objects and others are drawn to them. Some can appreciate them individually and others lump them all together. Some look carefully and others look but do not see.

For some students, the object exercise is maddening because they want to know what things are properly called. I will not tell the students what the objects are until the end of the exercise. I want the students to experience an act of imagination. If I do not know what something is for sure, what could it be? Sometimes we are so anxious for answers, we accept answers that make no sense or are wrong. We want to know what things are called because we want closure. Closure, though, is the end of thought. True enough that if we did not have closure about some things—like the names of things in our everyday world—we would go mad. The word chair, for instance, is ambiguous but it usually either means an object you sit on, the head of a department, or the death penalty. The choices are more or less limited. But if we work from the premise that what we do with objects we also do with people, we then get into some disturbing areas. For instance, sometimes a child displays a set of behaviors and is labeled attention deficient. Sometimes the label is true and the label helps everyone—including the child. Sometimes, however, the label is not true and creates harm. The child who is given this label may acquire the disability because he is treated as already having the condition. I do believe that our words create and I have seen very well-intentioned people work with children with disabilities and their language retards the children. If you speak to a child as retarded, you can retard him or her. The limitations are in the eyes of the speaker and not in the child. This example gets us into the realm of the self-fulfilling prophecy, which is very important to understand given how powerful it is. It is to this concept that I will now turn and I will end this discussion on perception with a skill that is equally powerful called the perception check.

The self-fulfilling prophecy speaks of the power of one's own thoughts. It is not magical thinking but everything does cycle back to how we think. The following quote is frequently attributed to Ghandi:

> Be careful what you think, for your thoughts become your words. Be careful what you say for your words become your actions. Be careful what you do, for your actions become your character. And your character is everything.

This quote makes clear the interrelatedness of all things. It is not typically the way we think because we tend to think in terms of separateness and disconnection. Other cultures see connections much more than we do. The quote asks us to contemplate the possibility that everything is connected. So having said that, here is how the self-fulfilling prophecy works: You have a particular thought. You act on that thought. You experience the truth of the original thought. It is not magic. Your action produces the truth of the claim but the claim starts with you. Let's look at some examples. Your friend invites you to a party and your perception is that everyone at the party is a snob. You go but you act unfriendly and aloof. If you act unfriendly and aloof, chances are that people will stay away from you. When people stay away from you, you may say: "See, I told you that everyone at the party is a snob." What you do not see is that you are the snob. This is an important idea that has far-reaching ramifications. It returns back to the idea that what we find in the world is what is inside us. We frequently do not understand that we are responsible for much of our own suffering. Here is another example that may hit home with some readers. You think that you are not smart so you do not apply yourself to your school work. You do not do the work so you eventually fail. Once you fail, you may say: "See, I told you that I was not smart." You forget that your action produced the result; it did not just happen.

So far, I have been speaking of the negative consequences of the self-fulfilling prophecy but it can work positively as well. You can tell yourself that you will learn something in school and then act in ways that will produce learning (being attentive, taking notes, doing the reading). Most likely, in this scenario you will learn. So often it is not the situation but ourselves that needs to change.

The self-fulfilling prophecy not only works with ourselves but works with others as well. Our ideas about others shape our behavior toward them and we make our ideas about others become true. I can think of no better example than the classroom. There was a study done where a class was arbitrarily divided along the lines of intelligence. The researcher split the class roster in two and told the teacher one group was intellectual gifted and the other group was intellectually challenged. The end-result was the children's performance fit into the group that they were arbitrarily assigned. The teacher's "knowledge" of the intelligence level of each student must have effected how she treated each student and then the treatment produced the results.[23] This study is referred to as the pygmalion effect referring to the play *Pygmalion* by George Bernard Shaw where a professor transforms a crude character into a refined lady.

I am especially concerned about how the self-fulfilling prophecy impacts children with disabilities. Many people see children with disabilities as not only different but as less than other children. Sometimes this mentality is even built in to a special education curriculum. I have seen well-intentioned therapists and teachers not expect anything from a child with disability and then, the child ends up not performing. It may not be that the child cannot perform and may have more to do with the perceptions of the teacher. I remember one of my students was speaking about a program where he worked which was supposed to teach life skills to people with disabilities. One day, the teachers were supposed to teach a cooking lesson to people with disabilities. My student observed how his boss did all the cooking but never taught the students how to cook. When he confronted her on this, she responded: "They are never going to learn how to do it." You may have once learned the expression: If you think you cannot do something, you are correct and if you think you can do something, you are also correct. The students in her class never had a chance to learn because of her perceptions of their capabilities.

I will make one last comment with regard to perception and people with disabilities. Most people define people with disabili-

---

[23] See Robert Rosenthal and Lenore Jacobson's *Pygmalion in the Classroom* (New York: Irvington Press, 1992).

ties by what they cannot do instead of what they can do. This deficit model of education is extremely destructive. Most models of education, for the average population, work on an accomplishment model. School mostly builds on what you know by constantly adding to it. This is sometimes not the case for people with disabilities. Frequently, they are defined by what they cannot do: cannot walk or cannot talk. Some people with disabilities are extremely skilled at connecting with people but that is not stressed. A music therapist once told me a story of being approached by a couple representing a non-for-profit group bringing the arts to children with disabilities. They called their program The Penguin Project because, as everyone knows, penguins are birds that cannot fly. The whole program, then, was built on the deficit model. The founders were stressing what the kids could not do, well-intentioned as it was, and therefore the music therapist told the founder that the kids were being set up to fail.

I do not frequently speak about skills because I believe that once you start to change your way of seeing communication, your skills will change as well. I will, however, teach the skill of the perception check. What is a perception check? A perception check works from the assumption that we all see the world differently. It allows us to speak about that which we see without getting defensive or making the other person feel defensive. There are three steps to the perception check. One, describe what you see. Two, generate as many points of view as you can (here is where imagination comes in). Three, ask the other person for agreement. So now let's look at what this would sound like. If you met with someone and you thought that their vision was short-sighted, you could say: it seems to me that you are building an entire program around what children cannot do. Are you stressing that penguins cannot fly when compared to other birds? Are you stressing that penguins can endure extreme temperatures that other birds cannot? Or are you stressing that they walk differently than other birds? What is it that you hope to achieve by calling the program this name and in reality, how do think it will serve children in the long run? I think that the perception check allows you to express what you see and may open up an area that the other did not think about.

Let's take another example. A woman I know, who was a Ph.D, went to see a new physician for a condition she had. She told the physician: "I am a doctor too." To her comment, the physician asked: "What is your area of specialty?" The woman answered: "Educational policy." The physician gave her a wave of the hand. My friend felt dismissed by the physician but said nothing. She told the physician that she was a doctor because she wanted to be spoken to on a certain level. She wanted the physician to speak to her as her equal. It backfired. Here, a perception check asks the physician to be accountable for her nonverbal communication. My friend could have said: "I feel that your gesture dismissed me. Did you do that because you feel the Ph.Ds are not real doctors? Did you do that because you think I am asking you to speak to me in such a way that I really will not understand? Are you impatient with patients asking you to explain things that you think they may not understand?" I may add that the word doctor means teacher so Ph.Ds may be more entitled to use the title than physicians or that physicians are really teachers. When you do the perception check, you cannot be sarcastic because that will come across and most likely, it will not go well because the other will react to the sarcasm.

I have used perception checks and the outcomes were very good. In order to use the perception check, you need to be very attentive during the communication transaction. You need to know how you are experiencing something in the moment. Some of us only understand what happened in a situation after we leave it. The more you practice being attentive and present in every conversation that you take part in, the more you will be able to identify your own and other people's intentions.

The act of celebration is thus one of memorialization. By words and rejoicing the beholder seeks to crystalize the nobility, the excellence, the sacredness fleetingly revealed.
Lawrence W. Rosenfield

Chapter VII

Acceptance, Gratitude, and Celebration

So far, I have been speaking about a certain way of being in the world. The way of being in the world is best characterized by an ancient Greek sensibility. This sensibility has been popularized by many contemporary writers but it has been around for a very long time. Sometimes students speak about the connections to the ideas presented in books like Rhonda Byrne's *The Secret*. Books like these are merely tapping into the same frame of reference. Frankl is tapping into this frame of reference as well. Gordon Alport, in his preface to Frankl's work states that the ideas he is presenting have been with us since the ancient Stoics as well as the modern existentialists.[24] I need to interject here the importance of studying the history of ideas. If we do not know where ideas come from, we think that ideas just one day appear. Most ideas are not invented but instead presented in a new and fresh way. Diane Glancy, in *Speaking the Corn into Being*, states that we breathe new life into words and therefore give ideas new breath. A modern-day example may help to explain. Several years ago, I did some consulting work for the fashion company Ralph Lauren. The owner of this company is seen as a master of marketing and merchandising. I started to do my own research on the invention of the department store and discovered

---

[24]In Frankl's *Man's Search for Meaning*, 12.

that all of the strategies use by Ralph Lauren were used at the turn of the century during the invention of the department store.[25]

It is important to remember our previous discussion of words when we encounter the words stoic and existential. Both come from a particular place in time and it is important to stop and look up the etymologies because if we do not do this, we do not know what the author is referring to. I find that most students do not stop and look up words when they read. Remember how this practice creates a self-fulfilling prophecy. Students say that they do not understand the works that they read. When asked they also say that they did not look up words. How can you understand if you do not know the vocabulary?

So before we go further, we need to provide a context for these words. Your research into the words can go as deep as you would like. A definition and the etymology will be found in a good dictionary. A more comprehensive search will include books like *The Encyclopedia of Philosophy* which will tell you how the words have evolved over the centuries. The word stoic, when we use it today, means someone who does not wear his/her emotions on his/her sleeves. The dictionary states that it describes someone who is seeming indifferent to or not effected by pain, joy, grief, or pleasure. The reason we have this definition, though, is because this was a school of thought in ancient Greece led by Zeno who believed that all occurrences are the result of divine will thereby they should be calmly accepted.[26] The word stoic comes from the Greek *stoa* meaning porch, the place where Zeno taught.

The link between stoicism and existentialism lies in the concept of acceptance. Existentialism is an idea that has been around for a very long time but it gained tremendous popularity in the 19th and 20th century. The idea centers around absolute freedom of the individual to make his or her own choices. With this freedom comes absolute responsibility on the part of the individual. Within this context, everything is our choice and there is no escaping it. We cannot blame anyone for our choices.

---

[25]This work is presented in an academic paper written by L. W. Rosenfield and Janet Farrell Leontiou, "Museus e Magazines: The Art of Display" edited by A. M. Barbosa in *Congreso Nationale de Pesquisadoires em Artes Plasticas*, Anais 96, vo. I, 1997.
[26]All of this information was found in The American Heritage Dictionary, New College Edition.

When we use words like stoic, we connect back to these worlds. Learning where the words come from, you may recognize a part of yourself. This is what it means to receive an education. You may identify yourself as being a stoic and you may come to understand yourself better within this larger context of the ancient world. This is what it means when we say that to become educated is to be led out of darkness.

Having talked about the words stoicism and existentialism, we can now return to the first idea of this chapter: acceptance. We cannot change how things are. Our job is to accept the world as it is. Sometimes students hear in this claim a level of passivity. Acceptance is anything but passive. It is something very active and something that needs our constant attention. It is not something we do then we are done with it. It is an ongoing process. You may have come to the position where you feel that you have accepted only to realize that life throws you a curveball and you are asked to accept again. I realize that the reason why I love teaching this course is because it gives me many opportunities to relearn the content.

If we return for a moment to the ancient Zeno, we can begin to understand Frankl a bit more. Remember that Zeno believed that everything that is given to us is given by divine force. This idea permeates Frankl's writing about the concentration camps. Frankl, nor Zeno, are masochists or victims. They are both saying that life consists of suffering. One can create meaning from the suffering and then the suffering has a purpose. Once the suffering has purpose, it is transformed. It may not be seen as suffering any longer but instead becomes a divine gift. We now circle back to the idea of perception because this requires a particular way of seeing. You may have already experienced that which I am describing. Have you ever seen someone get sick and then transform his/her entire life in a positive way because of the illness? Sometimes these people even say that the illness saved their lives. Remember we are working in the realm of perception, the person may even die but still feel grateful because he/she was given the opportunity to redeem oneself before death. Frankl writes of one woman who experiences this level of gratitude:

This young woman knew that she would die in the next few days. But when I talked to her she was cheerful in spite of this knowledge. "I am grateful that fate has hit me so hard," she told me. "In my former life I was spoiled and did not take spiritual accomplishments seriously."[27]

Not all example are as dramatic as the one described above. This mentality calls upon us to accept everything because in reality we have no other choice. You can fight reality but it is not a healthy way to live. This philosophy states optimism is the best choice; experiences are given to us and it is up to us how we make sense of them.[28] Frankl tells us that we should try to see things in the best possible light. He calls this a case for tragic optimism. Life is tragic, he tells us, but we should choose to be optimistic anyway. The word optimism comes from Latin *ops* meaning the god of abundance or plenty. Seeing abundance comes from a point of view and seeing scarcity also comes from a choice of a point of view. As Americans, most of us lead lives that are rich in terms of material wealth yet some are not satisfied and are always seeking more. Part of what it means to buy into a capitalist structure is that you will never be satisfied. Satisfaction comes from that allusive next purchase around the corner. We have been trained to see what we are missing instead of what we have been given.

Frankl states that we need to be worthy of our suffering. He quotes Dostoevsky on this point: "There is only one thing that I dread: not to be worthy of my suffering."[29] Frankl states something that seems extremely hopeful and encouraging. He states that even within a concentration camp, there was the opportunity to create something out of the suffering. Most readers will agree if people within a concentration camp can achieve this then the average person can accomplish this in his/her life. Frankl states: The words of Bismarck could be applied:

"Life is like being at the dentist. You always think that the worst is still to come, yet it is over already." Varying this, we could say that most men in a concentra-

---

[27]Frankl, *Man's Search for Meaning,* 90.
[28]Frankl, *Man's Search for Meaning,* 87.
[29]Frankl, *Man's Search for Meaning,* 87.

tion camp believed that the real opportunities of life had passed. Yet, in reality, there was an opportunity and a challenge. One could make a victory of those experiences turning life into an inner triumph, or one could ignore the challenge and simply vegetate, as did the majority of the prisoners.[29]

Here, of course, and throughout the book Frankl is not just talking about concentration camp prisoners but about us. We can look at what we have been given as a gift to take us to a higher level and therefore, become stronger or we can look at what we have been given as punishment and therefore, see ourselves as weak and as victims. The choice is clear and it is always our choice to make.

Frankl speaks about how one only knows one's own experience so therefore we cannot compare one experience to another. It may be helpful to discuss this point because when we are the one experiencing the suffering, it seems great and it seems to consume us. Frankl tells us that suffering is relative and he uses the analogy of gas to explain his point:

> If a certain quantity of gas is pumped into an empty chamber, it will fill the chamber completely and evenly, no matter how big the chamber. Thus suffering completely fills the human soul and the conscious mind, no matter whether the suffering is great or little. Therefore the "size" of human suffering is absolutely relative.[30]

This idea is one that I personally struggle with because of my own situation. As I have mentioned, I have a child with disabilities and watch how he and children like him struggle. Because I bear witness to this, it sometimes makes me impatient with others and what they perceive as suffering. For instance, I am of the age where many of my friends' children are moving away to college. Some lament that it is awful to let go of their children and see them

---

[29]Frankl, *Man's Search for Meaning,* 93.
[30]Frankl, *Man's Search for Meaning,* 64.

begin a life on their own. As I listen, I think that the parent is so fortunate to see the child grown, see the child being able to move on to higher education, and to know that the child will be able to stand on one's own two feet. I need to watch my own response because while the other sees the experience as bittersweet, I am only seeing how lucky the parent is to have this experience. I have this experience often and it is only because I see the world through the lens of disability. Frankl too, speaks about how he and the others could see life in a particular way after being released from the concentration camp. Frankl is walking with his friend as his friend starts to trample a field of green crops. Frankl states that no matter what happens to us, we never have permission to use our freedom in a way that destroys. Even, as in this example, he is talking about the life of plants:

> During this psychological phase one observed that people with natures of a more primitive kind could not escape the influences of the brutality which had surrounded them in camp life. Now, being free, they thought they could use their freedom licentiously and ruthlessly. The only thing that had changed for them was they now were the oppressors instead of the oppressed. They became instigators, not objects, of willful force and injustice. They justified their behavior by their own terrible experiences. This was often revealed in apparently insignificant events. A friend was walking across a field with me toward the camp when suddenly we came to a field of green crops. Automatically, I avoided it, but he drew his arm through mine and dragged me through it. I stammered something about not treading down the young crops. He became annoyed gave me an angry look and shouted, "You don't say! And hasn't enough been taken from us? My wife and child have been gassed—not to mention everything else—and you would forbid me to tread on a few stalks of oats!"[31]

---

[31] Frankl, *Man's Search for Meaning,* 112.

I copied this quote at length because it is important for all of us to realize that when we think we are lashing out against the harm that has been done to us, we are really just recreating the original damage. I was once giving a talk on the language of the medical system and a woman in the audience spoke of how her daughter was harshly treated as a medical intern. Now as the doctor, she is treating her own interns poorly. She tells her mother: "revenge is sweet." Revenge is not sweet. Revenge is perpetuating the misery and recreating it for the other and for yourself. As Frankl states, the doctor has merely switched places but is still operating within the same system. The doctor is now the oppressor instead of the oppressed.

Throughout this book, I want you to ask yourself what is it you wish to create? I am asking you to consciously choose what you now do automatically. Once you realize that you have choices, you realize that you are free. You will no longer be jerked around by people and circumstances. You can then shift out of the position of victim into being an autonomous human being. One reader stated that *Man's Search for Meaning* is: "The story of a man who became a number who became a person." This is Frankl's experience but we need not go through the same trajectory. We need not lose everything in order to gain something. We can learn how to appreciate what we have through his words. Sometimes, however, people do need to experience loss in order to gain. Think about this for yourself. Do you need to get sick to appreciate health? Do you need to lose a relationship in order to appreciate it? Sometimes we do need to learn through our own experience and sometimes we can learn through the experience of another.

Frankl, in his work, is cultivating a mind set that shares a common ground with the ancient Greeks. That mind set is to be appreciative of everything because everything you experience takes you to where you need to be. This mentally speaks about a trust. Whatever you call that entity is fine. For some, that entity will be called God and for others it may be called the universe. The Greeks would have said that our experiences were governed by the gods. Sometimes we get exactly what we need and sometimes the experience is extremely painful. We never would have chosen to experience the pain but it is necessary. The pain takes us where we need to go. Some theorists state that learning how to understand one's own suffering is the beginning of wisdom. I have always wished that we taught subjects like this in school. I have a theory that the most essential lessons in life are left out of the curriculum and everyone is left to reinvent the wheel alone. That is why I think Frankl is so essential.

At the end of *Man's Search for Meaning*, Frankl talks about a case for tragic optimism. What Frankl is saying is life is tragic. Bad things happen. According to Frankl, it is foolish to think of life any differently but we should choose to be optimistic anyway. He is saying what the ancients said: celebrate life. The ancients understood that we had the choice to celebrate life or disparage life and the choice we make determines how we live. It really is simple. We have all met people who live life as a cause of celebration. Everything about them grows out of this perception. On the opposite side, we have also met those who disparage life. For those people, nothing is enough because they are committed to their own unhappiness. It is not the circumstances that create their unhappiness but rather it is themselves that creates their own unhappiness. These people are miserable and their language is usually one of complaint. When speaking with others, these people usually look for those with whom they can commiserate. Have you heard the expression misery loves company? I speak about how sometimes people compete for the prize for being the most miserable. Is that really a competition that you wish to win? Most times, these people are oblivious to what they are creating with their speech. Oblivious means death; they are dead to an awareness of self.

The term hospitality, therefore, should not be limited to its literal sense of receiving a stranger in our house— although it is important never to forget or neglect that!—but it is a fundamental attitude toward our fellow human being, which can be expressed in a great variety of ways.

Henri J. M. Nouwen

Chapter VIII
The Self and the Other

The word interpersonal means between persons. In the previous chapter, I discussed how we choose to talk to others and in this chapter, I will begin to unpack how it is that we see others. It seems self-evident but it really is a complicated process. First, I like to use the language of host and guest to frame our discussion of how we see the other. The relationship of host and guest is a reciprocal one—sometimes I receive you and sometimes you receive me. We shift back and forth just like we do in conversation.

I will start with the word host and see what the word reveals because the word is there to instruct us. The word host is ambiguous. It can mean one who receives guests as in the word hospitality, hostess, and hospital. The word can also mean the opposite as one who receives enemies as in the words hostile, hostility, and hostage. The word host itself can mean hostile in the sense that you can serve as a host body when you are ill. A country may also serve as a host country meaning the physical location where a war is fought.

There is still a third meaning of the word and that is the eucharist. The eucharist is sometimes called the host and it refers to the body and blood of Christ. The word eucharist is Latin and it is very close to the Greek word for "I thank you." Phonetically, the Greek word is *evcharisto* which is very close to the Latin. It means that the eucharist, within a religious context, is an act of thanksgiving. The word gives us this insight. So given the three meanings of host, we may ask where does this leaves us? I think that the word itself tells us that we have a choice as to how to see the other. We can see the other as the enemy, the guest, or as divinity. The choice is ours. And the choice we make has more to do with how we see ourselves than how we see the other.

For some cultures, the vision of seeing the other as divine is built into their language. The word namaste means the god within me greets the god within you. Before we see the other as divine, however, we must see ourselves as divine. This concept has taken me a long time to understand and it may require some maturity before arriving at it. Psychologists use a term called projection to mean what we project on-to others what really belongs to us. If we are not comfortable with ourselves, we project that on-to others and see everyone we encounter as the enemy. We sometimes tell ourselves that this is the prudent way to be. I frequently encounter students who will say: "I am not going to speak in front of a bunch of strangers." The more a person does this, the more fearful the person becomes. Remember that whatever we choose to feed is what grows. When we feed our fears, they become stronger and when we feed our courage, it becomes stronger.

In an earlier chapter, I spoke about starting to choose responses instead of habitually falling into reactions. If you always stay away from the other, you are in reaction. You are not responding because if you were, you would not always act the same. You would act differently in each situation you encounter. You would also learn how to read each situation. If you know how you are going to behave before you arrive in each new situation, you are not thinking.

Each new situation requires our judgement. Judgement is a loaded word because we are frequently told not to judge others. I think that there is a difference between using judgment and being judgmental. Using judgment means discerning the difference between situations and the feelings that they provoke in you. I think that we need to learn how to pay attention to how we feel in the presence of the other. If you do not feel safe, for instance, I think that you need to pay attention to that feeling. This is what I mean by discernment. Being judgmental, on the other hand, is when we became small and dislike another for superficial reasons.

All too often, I see students with others who they should keep away and keeping away from others that should be embraced. Young women, right now, are very confused about who they should let in versus who they should keep away. Too many young women let in abusive boyfriends and keep out classmates who could genuinely offer them a sense of community. This is because the young women do not trust themselves. It always comes back to how we see ourselves.

Children are frequently told not to talk to strangers and the reason is that children lack the ability to judge. It is said that children do not develop into reasonable beings until the age of seven. Before that, they understand rules. The rule is: do not speak to strangers. We give children the rule because we think that they cannot treat each situation on its own terms. I remember once, a friend was visiting me with her four-year old son. I called the teapot design "stupid" and the little boy told his mother that I said a bad word. I tried to explain that calling the design of an object "stupid" is not the same thing as calling a person stupid. The little boy was not buying my argument. His mother looked at me and said: "It is the rule that we do not use that word. Let's just leave it at that." She was right.

There is, however, an underbelly to this discussion about children not frequently talked about. Sometimes children are abducted by strangers but sometimes when children are harmed, they are harmed within the house by someone they trust. If a child feels uncomfortable around someone that the family knows and trusts, the family may try to talk the child out of his/her feelings of discomfort. We sometimes teach a very distorted view of the world. Strangers are to be always be avoided and the family is to always be embraced. I have encountered students who were taught never to trust anyone outside the family. This has been the lesson in some families where the family members are stealing from each other and stabbing each other in the back.

Children are always in a separate category than adults. When I find students, at nineteen, who still do not talk to strangers I think that they are acting like children. They are developmentally stuck. Children do not bear the level of responsibility that we as adults do. Children frequently serve as scapegoats for adults. Scapegoating is when you blame another for something that really belongs to you. A parent may, for instance, feel that she or he did not accomplish much with her or his life and blame the children for one's own lack of achievement. Scapegoating allows the person to let himself or herself off the hook. It is a way of absolving oneself of responsibility. Sometimes grown children do this to their parents—most commonly, their mothers. Since this course speaks about radical responsibility, it is never acceptable to blame another for anything. It always comes back to choices that you have made. We tend to live in a culture that is always looking to blame outside factors and persons instead of shifting our focus to an individual's choices. We do each other a tremendous service when we ask each other to be accountable for individual choices and bear the consequences of those choices.

The word scapegoat is found in the Bible and it literally was a goat. The goat, symbolically, usually represents the devil. The priest would come into a community and hold up a goat. He would then ask the community members to transfer their sins to the animal. The animal would then be slaughtered thereby absolving the people of their sins. This is where the word comes from and we can see it at play on an individual level as well as a national level.

Those who serve as scapegoats on a national level usually are those with the least amount of power. Right now, we are going after undocumented workers within this country with a vengeance that really is frightening. Most people who are here illegally are trying to live the American dream. They are working hard, frequently doing jobs that Americans will not do, to support a family here and in their country of origin. We say that they are taking away jobs but we do not speak about how undocumented workers make our economy function. Many pay taxes and they spend money within our economy. Many businesses would not be able to function without them. We often say that things would be different had the immigrants entered our country through the appropriate channels. I think that this is naive on our part because there is no appropriate channel in many countries because the governments are thoroughly corrupt. The dark side of this story is that we are all immigrants and for many families, they came here however they could. Now, a similar access is being denied to those who come after us.

In this class, you are reading a book that is speaking about the aftereffects of war. The Jews, in Nazi Germany, were scapegoated. The Jews came to be seen as the other and as the problem. People do not need to resort of scapegoating when conditions are good. The reality was that the German economy was failing and the Jews were constructed as the cause for that failure. Hitler started to speak about the Jews as parasites. Once you start to see people as no longer being people, it is easier to entertain the idea of killing them. We need to always be on guard to speech that takes away a person's humanity. We tend to think that this no longer happens and that we have all learned our lesson from the Germans. This is not true. People frequently speak about prisoners as "animals." We say that it is different because the prisoner is guilty whereas the Jew was an innocent victim. I then point out that not everyone who is behind bars is guilty. Sometimes the difference between us and them is that they were caught and we were not or someone was even at the wrong place at the wrong time. The other issue is that even the guilty ones are still human beings and their despicable actions does not change that fact. By calling them animals, it cultivates a Nazi reaction that we can do to them whatever we please.

What I have been speaking about in this chapter may fall under the heading of xenophobia. Xenophobia means a fear of the other or the stranger. Xeni is a Greek word and it carries some of the ambiguilty of the Latin host. The *xeni,* in Greek, may be the enemy or the guest. It does not contain the element of the divine as does the word host. The word xenophobia speaks to the fact that we frequently project our own fears on-to anything or anyone who is strange to us. We are afraid of people who are different because we are afraid of the parts of ourselves that make us different.

As any child will tell you, it is very difficult to be different. Some people cannot hide their difference. They wear their difference of skin color, sexual orientation, or disability. Most see people who are different from them as less than. People of color, homosexuals, and people with disabilities have all fought to be given protection under the law and have worked to be seen as equals. I will speak here about people with disabilities because this topic is so close to me. People with disabilities are frequently seen as being less than people without disabilities. This does not have to be this way but this is the way we have constructed it. I refer to this as the deficient model. People with disabilities are seen as lacking what other people have. There is always a standard by which they are measured and they always come up lacking. I think that if you are a person with disabilities, you have frequently received messages from the culture that you are lacking. It is very difficult to grow up with a steady diet of these messages and maintain a healthy sense of self.

I once attended a forum where teenagers spoke about what it was like to go through life with a disability. One young man told the story of going to the zoo. He was alone in his wheelchair and a woman approached him with the comment: "What a pity that a good looking young man like you is in a wheelchair!" His response was: "Would you like it if I were ugly too?" This story demonstrates one of the strategies people with disabilities must use to deflect the comments that come their way. Humor, as this young man shows, is a very effective strategy. I am sure that the woman who approached this young man at the zoo thought she was being very kind to him. I see well-intentioned people talk to people with disabilities in ways that could retard them. This is because of a lack within the speaker; it has nothing to do with the person with disability. All of this stems from the fact that the speaker does not see the listener as equal.

This entire discussion of people with disabilities brings us back to where I began this chapter. When we speak to each other, we need to use our imaginations. We need to see each other, and ourselves, as divine. If I cannot see the other as divine it is usually because I cannot see myself as divine. I can choose to see the other as less than me because I need to put the other down so I can see myself as being in the one up position. If we speak in a way that degrades the other, we are announcing to the world how little we think of ourselves.

You know, I have come to think listening is love, that's what it really is.

Brenda Ueland

Chapter IX
Listening

In the previous chapter, I spoke about the importance of listening to oneself. Looked at another way, listening is the essence of hospitality extended to ourselves or to the other. Like most important aspects of life, few of us are taught how to listen. It is assumed that you know how to do it. The same could be said about communication in general. Communication is the most essential aspect of us yet we think that we do not need instruction or when there is instruction, we reduce listening to a technique and that destroys it.

I have previously written a book on medical communication. Since then, I have talked with medical doctors about communication within their field. Some doctors tell me that they train interns to ask the mother, who is sitting by her child's bedside in the hospital, about her night. As we had said before if you are asking a question because you have been instructed to, that intention will come through.

Let's first start with the word "listen." The word means to obey from below. The idea of humility is built into the word. Listening means that we lower ourselves so that we may attend to the other. Listening means that we attempt to remove our egos and try to see the world through someone else's point of view. Most of us know what it feels like when someone truly listens to us. It feeds us. Conversely, we know what it feels like when someone is going through the motions. We come away from these encounters feeling diminished.

Listening has a few aspects to it that are worthwhile discussing: attending, understanding, responding, and remembering. Attending means that you tune out all distractions and attend. In

71

the multitasking life most of us lead, this is easier said than done. It requires tremendous effort and discipline. Most of us are always doing something else while we are listening. Any wonder that we do not remember what we have been told? If we are not present, then we do not remember.

Understanding means to stand under. Here, again is the idea of humility. The word humility comes from humus meaning of the earth. When we have humility, we are grounded. When we try to understand, we make an attempt to enter a world that is not ours. As we have discussed, this requires an act of imagination. It takes imagination to try to see through different eyes. Without imagination, we cannot listen.

We have already discussed responding. To respond means to answer. Too often, we do not respond. When we do not respond, we miss an opportunity to feed the speaker. When we respond to the speaker, it is called feedback because we choose to feed the speaker. We can respond to the speaker in many different ways and each situation calls for a different response. This is why formulas do not work with communication. When I teach interviewing skills, my students ask me how to respond when the interviewer asks them a particular question. What they are asking is: what is the formula? Formulas have a way of backfiring. If you give a canned answer, the interviewer will know it and take it as a sign of disrespect toward him or her. Remember that each utterance contains information about the content and about the relationship. The interviewer will more likely than not think you are insulting his or her intelligence. Communication, within any context, is not supposed to be formulaic. I would even go so far to say that it is a formula, it is no longer communication. I am very disheartened when I see communication taught as formula.

The important thing to consider in responding is that you have choices. All too often, we fall into a rut. When someone speaks to us, we always respond in the same way. We frequently have more choices than we think we have. Here are some of the choices that are available to you: ask questions, offer analysis, offer judgment, empathize, sympathize, speak about yourself, give advice, or argue. Each response has pros and cons and each response needs to be appropriate to the situation. When we make the wrong choice, we end up being not very helpful to the speaker. Let's look at each response.

Asking good questions is an important skill to have. As the speaker, we can gain tremendous clarity for ourselves if our partner asks us good questions. The listener also gains understanding through asking questions. I am amazed at how infrequently we ask questions. Asking questions seems to be a lost art. I would also say that the investigative questions of who, what, when, where, and why are usually not insightful questions. Sometimes these types of questions, instead of taking you to the heart of the matter, serve to distract and frustrate. There have been occasions, for instance, when a student discloses in the class that he has been to prison. The students want to ask the investigative questions which I prohibit because I do not think that they are important. Within this context, I think that the only important question is: what have you learned?

Offering analysis at the right time and at the right place is an excellent response. Offering analysis, when it is not right, alienates the speaker and makes them feel like you are playing psychologist. When we offer analysis, we may call our partner's attention to something that is outside his/her realm of consciousness. For instance when a friend is telling you about some difficulty, you may call to her attention that this is a familiar pattern for her. Remember that whatever you speak, it needs to be for the other and not for yourself. It also needs to be spoken with love. If you speak because you want to sound superior, that intention will always come through.

Offering judgment can be extremely helpful but not if you sound judgmental. I remember that when my twins were born, I was complaining that everyone needed me. "Even the cat needs me," I complained to my brother. "Right," my brother said, "and there is something wrong with everyone needing you?" My brother offered a judgment and it was just what I needed at the time. Sometimes other's judgments allow us to shift our point of view. Sometimes it is painful but sometimes it is necessary.

Responding with empathy is another choice. We said earlier that all we want is for others to get us and this is what an empathetic reponse offers. I know that for myself when a friend tells me that she understands, with sincerity, I feel my whole body start to relax. Understanding is a major component of listening and I think that to find people who understand us is rare. It is rare because it takes time, requires the listener to step outside oneself, and it requires concentration. All of these are rare commodities. Many us just make believe that we understand when we do not. Sometimes we do this because we do not want to expose our lack of understanding or we do not have the interest (or energy) to try to understand. Many times, we are looking for an empathetic response from our listener when we speak.

Sometimes people confuse empathy with sympathy. They both share the Greek root of pathos which means feeling. Empathy, though, is a feeling between equals whereas sympathy places the other in a position lower than the other. Sympathy sometimes entails pity and sometimes it entails superiority. It is a feeling of pity for another and a secret gratitude that you are not the other. At times, the speaker is looking for sympathy and the worst thing that you, as the listener, can do is give it to her. I say "her" because more females play "the poor thing" than do males although some men play it too. When we give "the poor thing" sympathy, we are feeding her sense of helplessness. Psychologists would call us enablers because we enable the other to be helpless.

When you are in the role of listener, it is tricky because sometimes it is extremely helpful to speak about yourself and sometimes it is perceived as ambushing the conversation. I know someone in my life that no matter what I begin talking about, it always ends up being about her. This is frustrating and makes me not want to talk to her. I have another friend who never does this. When I talk about my kids, we never end up talking about her kids instead. I think that this is because of a conscious effort on my friend's part. It is always a fine dance and we all need to learn the moves between us so that we can discern what the other needs.

When I speak about giving advice as a response in listening, I have to speak about gender differences. Many men, when they listen, give advice and then end up getting into trouble. There is much to say about giving advice and I need to provide some context about men and women. Women, it seems, talk to establish connection and rapport. Women also speak to know their own minds. This has been brought out in the research[32] and I can confirm it through my own experience as a female. Speaking for me is

[32]Some examples of works on gender communication are: Deborah Tannen *You Just Don't Understand: Men and Women in Conversation* (NY: HarperCollins, 2001) and Robin Lakoff *Language and Woman's Place* (NY: Harper & Row, 1975).

a way to understand myself. When I talk, I think out loud. Men, generally speaking, (and I need to trust the research on this) do not use language this way. Men think their thoughts and then use language to report those thoughts. Given this difference, we run into problems when we try to communicate with one another. The woman, in trying to understand herself, starts to talk about a problem she is having and the man, thinking he would be seeking advice, offers advice. The woman invariably then becomes angry with the man. The man then is usually confused and may walk away thinking that women are confounding beings. It really is a clash in how the genders use language.

Many men are raised to fix things so when the woman in their life comes to them with a problem, he thinks that she must be asking him to fix it. I also think that most men want to help to make things better and they think that is a way to do it. It, unfortunately, frequently makes things worse. I frequently say in class that men and women are a match made in hell; women's complaint about men is that they do not listen and men's complaint against women is that they talk too much. At times, when I do listening exercises in the classroom, I tell the men that they can respond any way they wish but they cannot offer advice. Some men, when given this constraint, cannot respond at all.

When we want to offer advice, we need to make sure that we fully understand the situation. We also need to ask ourselves if the other wants advice or is ready to hear the advice from us. Sometimes asking the other is a trap and we as the listeners need to be cautious. If we give advice and the advice does not work out, we can be blamed. This may have been the reason why we were asked in the first place. It may be a strategy used for the other to avoid personal responsibility.

The last response that I will talk about is argument. We all know people who want to argue. Unfortunately, in my own experience I have found that lawyers frequently want to argue. I think that this is because it is their habit. Their way of being in the world is by bumping up against others. Argument is an important skill to have but it should not be used all the time. Plato said that argument was the seventh greatest intellectual ability. If you want to be good at constructing arguments, then you need to be a wonderful listener. So often people who wish to argue are not listening at all. Remember, also, you need to pay attention to intention. Argument for the sake of argument will never work in one's favor. The only authentic reason to enter into argument is to seek truth and to enter in purely, each party must be willing to give up his/her position.

Sometimes students want to argue in the classroom and frequently, these arguments are transparent. The intention is rarely seeking truth but has more to wanting to challenge the professor, wanting to insert one's own ego in the conversation, or wanting to derail the entire talk. The professor who is paying attention will usually pick up on the intention even if the speaker is not aware of it. I also need to say here that argument is not the same as fighting. What we mostly see is people fighting where they call each other names and each works to degrade the other. Argument, in contrast, is an academic discipline built upon reason and proof. It goes back to the times of the ancient Greeks when people, in developing a democracy, experimented with how to persuade and influence people without resorting to threats and violence. It should be noted that to enter the realm of violence is to abandon all communication. Violence is not another form of communication; they are two separate things.

From all this we may learn that there are two races of men in this world, but only these two—the "race" of the decent man and the "race" of the indecent man.

Viktor E. Frankl

Chapter X

Conclusion

I thought that I could conclude by offering a dichotomy. On one side of the dichotomy is how we act when we act out of habit and on the other side is the shift I ask in this book. Now that you have worked your way through the book and through the class. I hope that these lists make sense.

POINTS OF VIEW IN THE OLD WORLD VIEW:
1. We treat everything as a technique to be mastered.
2. We act like prison camp inmates.
3. We avoid responsibility by saying that we have been conditioned.
4. We adhere to a "dog-eat-dog" mentality.
5. We are fearful of taking initiative.
6. We do accept our own responsibility.
7. We are product driven and as a consequence, we are deeply unsatisfied.
8. We act entitled instead of grateful.
9. We have a schizophrenic relationship with the self; we feel both entitled and not worthy.
10. We speak in ways that maintain the status quo.
11. We put others down because our sense of self is so fragile. We try, therefore, to pump ourselves up but this is futile.
12. We seek out others with whom we can be miserable thereby recreating and reinforcing our misery.
13. We see ourselves as victims.
14. We do what we have always done expecting outcomes to be different.

15. We ask the world to adjust to us.
16. We act as if the world owes us a living.
17. We see violence is another form of communication.

The above list represents how we were. This new list, hopefully, encapsulates the shift that we have made over the course of the semester.

POINTS OF VIEW IN THE NEW WORLD VIEW:
1. Accept that to fully learn and become educated, we need to be led out of the darkness with humility.
2. Realize that we are beings of infinite potential and absolute freedom.
3. Know that everything is our choice.
4. We "feed" others with our words.
5. Trust ourselves, and by extension trust others.
6. Understand the honor in accepting responsibility.
7. Engage with the process and let go of connecting to end results.
8. Know that everything we have been given is a gift.
9. Have an appreciative attitude toward ourselves.
10. Begin to speak authentically.
11. Have our speech become benedictions. The word benediction is Latin and it means to give blessings and to speak well of.
12. Seek out those with whom we can celebrate.
13. See ourselves as causal agents; see ourselves as those who make things happen in our lives.
14. Use our imaginations so that we have an abundance of choices.
15. Know that every situation is an opportunity for us to grow, learn and adapt.
16. Know that the world owes us nothing. It is we who owe the world everything.
17. Know that to enter into violence is to abandon communication.

Chapter XI
Speaking the corn into being

By Diane Glancy

1 **M**y concept of the word, the spoken word, is an image I 1
have. It goes back to the time before we killed the word.
Before we put it in its little coffin, which the written
form is. When the word was alive. When it was spirit. When what
we spoke coordinated conditions (brought into harmony arrow
and animal). Or what we spoke actually served as a causal function. Words as transformers. As makers of things that happened.

Now this is the Cherokee understanding of the spoken word,
the voice, anyway. In our tradition, people do not simply speak
about the world, they speak the world into being. What we say
is intricately intertwined with what we are and can be. To the
Cherokee people, all things in the world have a voice—and that
voice carries life. Storying gives shape to meaning. This concept
of speech and voice is based on a notion that the voice does not
speak alone, but generations of voices speak. They must be heard
and understood by others and added onto by them. When we
speak we take the power of the spoken word and infuse it with
new breath. We add our voice to story so it shifts, changes, renews
with the multiplicity of meanings and the variables of possibilities.
To keep words alive and elastic. To keep them the shape-changers
they have to be for our survival.

The voice and the thought that rides upon the voice are the
challenge. What you speak is spoken into an energy field or field
of force that has consequence. The breath forming words is holy.
The sound and shape of them breathed into being.

The Cherokee knew their words had the power to create.
That's also the guardian, the check and balance, of the word. Its

From The West Pole *(University of Minnesota Press, 1997). The essay originally appeared in*
Freeing the First Amendment *(© New York University Press, 1995).*

power to generate force. What you said could last for generations. Therefore you guarded your words. You made them count in the oral tradition. You spoke them responsibly. You kept in mind that what the speaker says affects the speaker as much as the spoken to.

5 Now this is what I have to say about speaking the corn into 5 being.

In the old days the farmers did not know the day of planting. It was announced by the holy men. Then the orators would come and sing the seed corn into the field and the field into the form from which the corn would rise in the process of the seeds breaking. Then someone, usually the grandmother, would sit on her platform speaking the crows away from the seeded fields until the seeds were established in stalks and corn tassels waving and the corn itself could speak the crows away. The corn was mixed with words all summer. The fields were never without sound. Even after harvest, a green-corn ceremony honored the new crop. During the storing process. Even during baking or cooking, a woman would speak to the corn. Tell it stories. There was an interconnectedness of things.

Some of the Cherokee were evangelized by Christian missionaries. They found similarities in Yahweh and the Great Spirit because the Judeo-Christian God also spoke the world into being. He had the power to join mind and word. He knew the wholeness of being. In fact, there are stories that the Great Spirit made us because he wanted to share that power. He mixed us with the dust of the ground and his breath. It's breath that gives us kinship with the Great Spirit. Breath is in the sacredness of the spoken word. In turn, we are creators when we speak.

We are accountable for our words.

Chapter XII
The Stranger Within

Helen M. Luke

The American Heritage Dictionary tells us that the Indo-European root of the words "host," "hospice," "hospitality," and "hospital" is *ghosti*; it is, surprisingly, also the root of the word "guest." Moreover, in the Indo-European Appendix the meaning of this root includes another word: *ghosti* meant "stranger" as well as "guest" and "host," properly, "someone with whom one has reciprocal duties of hospitality." There follows yet another meaning: from this root word also came the English "hostile," via the second meaning of "host" as a multitude—often of enemies. This, again, is connected to the fear of the unknown, which leads to the frequent projection of suspicion and hostility onto anything or any person that is strange to us.

Russell Lockhart, in his splendid book *Words as Eggs*,[1] has said that behind every word that we use—for the most part so casually—there lies a story to be found, if we are willing to attend to its inner meaning. There is a level on which the essential story will be the same for all seekers, but also a level where it will be unique for every one of us. As the pattern of every snowflake is unique, so also are the stories that nourish every single human life.

Most men and women who seek wholeness, or in Dante's words, "the love that moves the sun and the other stars," will easily recognize consciously the outer duties of hospitality whether as host or guest (I hope that throughout this bit of writing, readers will know that in this context "host" includes both genders, so that they will not accuse me of ignoring the hostess! The word "host" transcends gender). However, the degree to which we live the beauty and courtesy of the exchanges between hosts

---

1. Dallas: Spring Publications. 1963

Reprinted from *Kaleidoscope: The Way of Woman and Other Essays* (1992), by permission of Apple Farm Community.

and guests, particularly when we are strangers to one another, will surely depend on our attitude to those inner images which are either the guiding truths of our lives, or, especially while they remain wholly unconscious or repressed, the controlling addictions or hidden goals of the psyche.

Imagination in its fundamental meaning, as defined by Shakespeare or Blake, and known to all great creative artists, is the making and the responding to images of all kinds in the outer and the inner worlds. We don't have to be great artists to do this; every one of us has the ability to respond by at least beginning to say "yes" or "no" to the strangers who knock on the doors of our souls. Even if our clear and honest response is "I am too weak to confront this threatening hostile stranger. I am as I am." That too may be the saving humility that admits the divine and transforming guest; but to shut one's ears and eyes and ignore the knocking within delivers the ego over to possession by the demand for security or power, from which is born anger, violence, and hardness of heart. How easy it then is to be blind to the needs of those we meet— especially if they are personalities who irritate or bore us—because only a truly imaginative response can keep us aware of the effect on the other of an insensitive lack of warmth in our welcome.

5   I have had considerable experience with the messages that 5 come to us through dreams. The voice of the dream will either warn of dangers in our attitudes to the journey of life or else give us courage as it points the way to new awareness. Thus we are enabled to take up the responsibilities of joy and so to find the kind of imaginative exchange which heals and unites. A very common theme in the dreams of someone who is unconsciously resisting a new awareness of such a responsibility, evading some hidden creative ability in him or herself, is that of a burglar or terrifying unknown person, or even a monster, who has broken into the house or is trying to get in to steal or perhaps to kill. The dreamer is often terrified and trying desperately in the dream to call the police, or find some means of evasion or escape from the intruder and so banish the threat to his or her inner security. Sometimes, as M. L. von Franz has written in one of her fairy tale books, it is *necessary* for the one threatened to run away. Much discrimination is needed to recognize these occasions.

However, more often when the stranger takes this form, it becomes clear that the unknown, or as yet rejected, new attitude has turned dangerously negative and threatening, determined to make itself felt. If the dreamer is able in imagination to turn the dream into a story, into which he or she actively enters, opening the door perhaps and confronting the intruder, asking what his need is, inviting him in as one would a guest, then a conversation may ensue, a recognition, a lessening of fear. Gradually if the dreamer truly attends and does not just forget it all after a day or two, the changed attitude begins to alter behavior, and even leads to a long resisted major change in the way of life. Thus do one's personal images bring to mind the great stories in the myths.

We remember that among so-called primitive people a stranger who came to the door of tent or home, seeking shelter and food, was to be welcomed as an honored guest, especially because so easily he might be a god in disguise, even if he could also be a disguised enemy. We may also remember those saints or sages in all the great religious traditions who would invite an obvious thief to take any of their possessions and make no effort to oppose him—and, more delightful still, the many hermits, and indeed the great naturalists of our own time, who realize they are guests, as it were, of the wild animals into whose land they intrude, and who treat them with respect and love and so are not threatened by them. As an example, I saw a program on PBS recently in which the white wolf mother of a pack on Ellesmere Island (in the Arctic, north of Canada) positively invited the man (whose name, I regret, I have forgotten) who had been living there in a tent for many months, to enter her den and see her new cubs. The exchanges of true hospitality were between them.

It is sad when we compare this to the almost universal collective behavior of civilized man as he explored new lands in search of power or wealth. Any thought of being a guest of those races who had lived there for thousands of years came only to the very few, and it may be that the worst damage of all was done by those who, with excellent intentions, tried to "rescue" their hosts from their ancient traditions and ways of life. Nevertheless, as always, there are the shining stories of great individuals—travellers and explorers—in whom the respect and courtesy of the true guest and host stand out and the patient interest of "reciprocal hospitality" has brought about a final trust even after centuries of hostility.

To mention one example among many in our own time, Laurens van der Post's books about his search for the remnants of the Bushmen—the first men of Africa—are a constant joy, recreating in the reader glimpses of the power and beauty of this latent spirit of hospitality in all the true meetings of our inner or outer lives.[2]

More than fifty years ago, I myself had the great good fortune to experience with my husband the extraordinarily gracious and spontaneous hospitality of a small group of Bedouin in the desert beyond Aman in Jordan when our car broke down. It was near sunset and we were welcomed into the young sheik's tent, given water to wash with, fed with specially prepared food, and entertained in every way they could devise without a shared language, as we waited for a mechanic, fetched by one of their young men who was sent on foot to the nearest village. Night fell and the stars shone out in the clear desert air while camels sat around resting. We were even offered a night's shelter. The experience left a living memory of the essential courtesy to the stranger in a strange land—a welcome with no hidden demand for any return, no questions asked—a free giving and taking of the simplest kind.

10 Perhaps it is because of this memory that the great story in our 10 own tradition that stands out for me as of a particular power when we turn to the very difficult task of creating this kind of simple guest and host exchange with the unknown aspects of ourselves, is the story of the coming of three men to Abraham in his old age (he was 99) as he sat at the entrance to his desert tent. After he had welcomed them and brought them water and food, the strangers asked him where his wife Sarah was, and then told them both that she would conceive and bear him a child. But Sarah laughed to herself, thinking them foolish, knowing that it was impossible at her age. And the guest (who had become one it seems, instead of three, and was indeed Yahweh himself) asked, "Why did Sarah laugh . . . is anything too wonderful for Yahweh?" "I did not laugh," said Sarah, lying because she was afraid. But he replied, "Oh, yes, you did laugh."

However, "Yahweh dealt kindly with Sarah . . . and did what he had promised her"—in spite of her somewhat contemptuous

---

2. Sir Laurens van der Post, *The Lost World of the Kalahari, The Heart of the Hunter,* both published by Harcourt, Brace and Jovanovich.

laughter at such nonsense. So Sarah conceived and bore a son to Abraham in his old age. And then comes the altogether delightful ending to the story. Then Sarah said, "God has given me cause to laugh; all those who hear of it will laugh with me."[3] From the laughter of rejection she has brought to birth the child and found the laughter at the heart of life in which all with ears to hear may join.

So it can be with all those strange and seemingly hostile or meaningless images that knock at our doors, either in dreams or in irrational moods, in emotions or cravings, in unnoticed use of words or habits of movement, both physical and psychic. If we dream we may experience all these habits and unconscious patterns already personified (though of course one needs a guide). If that is not our way, we can allow our imagination to do the same for them, and we may recognize them perhaps in our projections on to others, and then we may treat them all as the strange and unknown guests within who may have been wandering without food or water—that is, starving or withering from lack of acceptance, growing hostile and angry, and so shaking us awake. Then indeed we discover that they bring us a message from the Spirit within, from the Self, the God of innumerable names, the I Am That I Am. The message is a birth in us—even a rebirth of the inner child—a newness of life and laughter, no matter how impossible that may seem, as the stranger brought the child to Sarah in her old age.

In all the stories the emphasis is on food and drink—always symbols of the kind of attention and concern which is the essence of hospitality. The guest is to be offered nourishment on every level—nourishment of the kind we all need—the best we can offer—emphatically not our own concept of what is "good for" the other, including the other within. It is easy to forget that only to the extent that we listen and attend to these figures who express our own weaknesses and potential strengths have we any hope of recognizing in all those we meet in the outer world, either their needs as guests to be honored by us whether we like them or not, or their dues as hosts as they offer to us their acceptance and trust. We may find it hard to personify these unconscious denizens of the psyche; but mere "good" resolutions never change anything fundamentally. Shakespeare tells us that "the lunatic, the

---

3. Translations are from the Jerusalem Bible.

lover and the poet are of imagination all compact."[4] Within us
these strangers bring the divine guest who transforms us, often
through simple and unnoticed actions. That doesn't mean that we
must necessarily write poetry or paint pictures, but simply allow
the "poet" within us to give "a local habitation and a name"[5] to
our strange inner guests. When the reciprocal rules of hospitality
have become a spontaneous and joyful reality in the soul, then the
divine spark will live between the individual and the other in all
her or his meetings with every form of life.

Although it is so well known, I want to end with some brief
quotations from that story, beloved among all the Greek myths—
the tale of Baucis and Philemon, as told by the Roman poet Ovid
in his *Metamorphoses,* and translated by the American poet Rolfe
Humphries. Humphries' translation conveys to us in our own
language, with sheer delight, the spontaneous essence of true
hospitality, as Ovid describes the actions of two souls who have
grown into the simplicity of that love which no abstract words can
describe—the love in which mind and heart and instinct are at
one in the web of life, in time and in eternity.

15   Ovid describes how Jupiter and Mercury, disguised as mortals, 15
travelled the earth looking for rest.

> . . . They found a thousand houses
> Shut in their face. But one at last received them
> A humble cottage thatched with straw and reeds,
> A good old woman, Baucis, and her husband
> A good old man, Philemon, used to live there.
> They had married young, they had grown old together
> In the same cottage; they were very poor,
> But faced their poverty with cheerful spirit
> And made its burden light by not complaining,
> It would do you little good to ask for servants
> Or masters in that household, for the couple
> Were all the house; *both* gave and followed orders.
> So, when the gods came to this little cottage,
> Ducking their heads to enter, the old man
> Pulled out a rustic bench for them to sit on,
> And Baucis spread a homespun cover for it.

4. Shakespeare, *A Midsummer Night's Dream,* Act IV. Scene 1.
5. *Ibid*

There is no male superiority in this house! Ovid goes on to describe the kindling of the fire, blown on by Baucis, who hadn't much breath to spare in her old age; the cooking in a copper kettle of the cabbage brought in from their well-watered garden by Philemon, and a chunk of their precious side of bacon. And they made conversation

> To keep the time from being too long . . .
> Baucis, her skirts tucked up, was setting the table
> With trembling hands. One table leg was wobbly,
> A piece of shell fixed that.

20 The food is described, cottage cheese and eggs. The earthenware 20
and the wine "of no particular vintage"

> . . . and apples in wide baskets—
> Remember how apples smell?—and purple grapes
> Fresh from the vines, and a white honeycomb
> As centerpiece, and all around the table
> Shone kindly faces, nothing mean or poor
> Or skimpy in good will.

Then they noticed that the mixing bowl kept filling up all by itself and that scared them and they thought anxiously that their food wasn't good enough for such guests and wanted to kill their precious goose who was a sort of watchdog for them. But the goose ran to the gods and they revealed themselves, preventing the killing, and took the old couple up the mountain from which they saw that the houses in the valley whose doors had been closed to strangers were now flooded with water—all except their cottage. "And while they wondered they wept a little for their neighbors' troubles." Their cottage was now turning into a temple, and Jupiter asked them what they would like for themselves.

> . . . And they hesitated,
> Asked, could we talk it over just a little?
> And talked together apart.

Then Philemon spoke for both and asked that they might be priests having care of the temple and that they might die in the same hour.

25   And one day as they stood before the temple   25
    Both very old, talking the old days over
    Each saw the other put forth leaves.
    Philemon
    Watched Baucis changing. Baucis watched Philemon
    And as the foliage spread, they still had time
    To say "Farewell, my dear" . . .
    The peasants in that district still show the stranger
    The two trees close together, and the union
    Of oak and linden in one.

The beautiful ending of this story is a simple, natural image of the "hierosgamos," the final unity, the marriage of the opposites in which duality is transcended yet each partner remains unique— the oak and the linden remain themselves as their roots and branches intertwine in a single tree of life. The two old people had become hosts and guests to each other in their daily lives, and so to all life—to the gods and to all the unknown who came to their temple to honor and worship the divine images in their own hearts.

Ovid ends his poem by telling how he himself had seen this tree—one and yet still two—and brought a garland and said a verse:

"The gods look after good people still, and cherishers are cherished."

Chapter XIII
Tell me more

On the fine art of listening

I want to write about the great and powerful thing that listening is. And how we forget it. And how we don't listen to our children, or those we love. And least of all—which is so important too—to those we do not love. But we should. Because listening is a magnetic and strange thing, a creative force. Think how the friends that really listen to us are the ones we move toward, and we want to sit in their radius as though it did us good, like ultraviolet rays.

This is the reason: When we are listened to, it creates us, makes us unfold and expand. Ideas actually begin to grow within us and come to life. You know how if a person laughs at your jokes you become funnier and funnier, and if he does not, every tiny little joke in you weakens up and dies. Well, that is the principle of it. It makes people happy and free when they are listened to. And if you are a listener, it is the secret of having a good time in society (because everybody around you becomes lively and interesting), of comforting people, of doing them good.

Who are the people, for example, to whom you go for advice? Not to the hard, practical ones who can tell you exactly what to do, but to the listeners: that is, the kindest, least censorious, least bossy people that you know. It is because by pouring out your problem to them you then know what to do about it yourself.

When we listen to people there is an alternating current and this recharges us so that we never get tired of each other. We are constantly being re-created. Now there are brilliant people who cannot listen much. They have no ingoing wires on their apparatus. They are entertaining, but exhausting, too. I think it is because these lecturers, these brilliant performers, by not giving us a chance to talk, do not let us express our thoughts and expand; and it is this little creative fountain inside us that begins to spring and cast up new thoughts and unexpected laughter and wisdom. That is why, when someone has listened to you, you go home rested and lighthearted.

5   Now this little creative fountain is in us all. It is the spirit, or 5 the intelligence, or the imagination—whatever you want to call it. If you are very tired, strained, have no solitude, run too many errands, talk to too many people, drink too many cocktails, this little fountain is muddied over and covered with a lot of debris. The result is you stop living from the center, the creative fountain, and you live from the periphery, from externals. That is, you go along on mere will power without imagination.

It is when people really listen to us, with quiet fascinated attention, that the little fountain begins to work again, to accelerate in the most surprising way.

> If you are a listener,
> everybody around you
> becomes lively and
> interesting.

I discovered all this about three years ago, and truly it made a revolutionary change in my life. Before that, when I went to a party I would think anxiously: "Now try hard. Be lively. Say bright things. Talk. Don't let down." And when tired, I would have to drink a lot of coffee to keep this up.

Now before going to a party, I just tell myself to listen with affection to anyone who talks to me, *to be in their shoes when they talk;* to try to know them without my mind pressing against theirs, or arguing, or changing the subject. No. My attitude is: "Tell me more. This person is showing me his soul. It is a little dry and meager and full of grinding talk just now, but presently he will begin to think, not just automatically to talk. He will show his true self. Then he will be wonderfully alive."

10   Sometimes, of course, I cannot listen as well as others. But 10 when I have this listening power, people crowd around and their heads keep turning to me as though irresistibly pulled. It is not because people are conceited and want to show off that they are drawn to me, the listener. It is because by listening I have started up their creative fountain. I do them good.

Now why does it do them good? I have a kind of mystical notion about this. I think it is only by expressing all that is inside that purer and purer streams come. It is so in writing. You are taught in school to put down on paper only the bright things. Wrong. Pour out the dull things on paper too—you can tear them up afterward—for only then do the bright ones come. If you hold back the dull things, you are certain to hold back what is clear and beautiful and true and lively.

So it is with people who have not been listened to in the right way—with affection and a kind of jolly excitement. Their creative fountain has been blocked. Only superficial talk comes out—what is prissy or gushing or merely nervous. No one has called out of them, by wonderful listening, what is true and alive.

I think women have this listening faculty more than men. It is not the fault of men. They lose it because of their long habit of striving in business, of self-assertion. And the more forceful men are, the less they can listen as they grow older. And that is why women in general are more fun than men, more restful and inspiriting.

Now this non-listening of able men is the cause of one of the saddest things in the world—the loneliness of fathers, of those quietly sad men who move among their grown children like remote ghosts. When my father was over 70, he was a fiery, humorous, admirable man, a scholar, a man of great force. But he was deep in the loneliness of old age and another generation. He was so fond of me. But he could not hear me—not one word I said, really. I was just audience. I would walk around the lake with him on a beautiful afternoon and he would talk to me about Darwin and Huxley and Higher Criticism of the Bible.

15 "Yes, I see, I see." I kept saying and tried to keep my mind 15 pinned to it, but I was restive and bored. There was a feeling of helplessness because he could not hear what I had to say about it. When I spoke I found myself shouting, as one does to a foreigner, and in a kind of despair that he could not hear me. After the walk, I would feel that I had worked off my duty and I was anxious to get him settled and reading in his Morris chair, so that I could go out and have a livelier time with other people. And he would sigh and look after me absentmindedly with perplexed loneliness.

For years afterward I have thought with real suffering about my father's loneliness. Such a wonderful man, and reaching out to me and wanting to know me! But he could not. He could not listen. But now I think that if only I had known as much about listening then as I do now, I could have bridged that chasm between us. To give an example:

Recently, a man I had not seen for 20 years wrote me: "I have a family of mature children. So did your father. They never saw him. Not in the days he was alive. Not in the days he was the deep and admirable man we now both know he was. That is man's life. When next you see me, you'll just know everything. Just your father all over again, trying to reach through, back to the world of those he loves."

Well, when I saw this man again, what had happened to him after 20 years? He was an unusually forceful man and had made a great deal of money. But he had lost his ability to listen. He talked rapidly and told wonderful stories and it was just fascinating to hear them. But when I spoke—restlessness: "Just hand me that, will you? . . .Where is my pipe?" It was just a habit. He read countless books and was eager to take in ideas, but he just could not listen to people.

Well, this is what I did. I was more patient—I did not resist his non-listening talk as I did my father's. I listened and listened to him not once pressing against him, even in thought, with my own self-assertion. I said to myself: "He has been under a driving pressure for years. His family has grown to resist his talk. But now, by listening, I will pull it all out of him. He must talk freely and on and on. When he has been really listened to enough, he will grow tranquil. He will begin to want to hear me."

20   And he did, after a few days. He began asking me questions. 20 And presently I was saying gently:

"You see, it has become hard for you to listen."

He stopped dead and stared at me. And it was because I had listened with such complete, absorbed, uncritical sympathy, without one flaw of boredom or impatience, that he now believed and trusted me, although he did not know this.

"Now talk," he said. "Tell me about that. Tell me all about that."

Well, we walked back and forth across the lawn and I told him my ideas about it.

25   "You love your children, but probably don't let them in. Un- 25 less you listen, people are wizened in your presence: they become about a third of themselves. Unless you listen, you can't know anybody. Oh, you will know facts and what is in the newspapers and all of history perhaps, but you will not know one single person. You know, I have come to think listening is love, that's what it really is."

Well, I don't think I would have written this article if my notions had not had such an extraordinary effect on this man. For he says they have changed his whole life. He wrote me that his children at once came closer; he was astonished to see what they are; how original, independent, courageous. His wife seemed really to care about him again, and they were actually talking about all kinds of things and making each other laugh.

For just as the tragedy of parents and children is not listening, so it is of husbands and wives. If they disagree they begin to shout louder and louder—if not actually, at least inwardly—hanging fiercely and deafly onto their own ideas, instead of listening and becoming quieter and quieter and more comprehending. But the most serious result of not listening is that worst thing in the world, boredom: for it is really the death of love. It seals people off from each other more than any other thing. I think that is why married people quarrel. It is to cut through the non-conduction and boredom. Because when feelings are hurt, they really begin to listen. At last their talk is a real exchange. But of course, they are just injuring their marriage forever.

Besides critical listening, there is another kind that is no good: passive, censorious listening. Sometimes husbands can be this kind of listener, a kind of ungenerous eavesdropper who mentally (or aloud) keeps saying as you talk: "Bunk . . . Bunk . . . Hokum."

Now, how to listen? It is harder than you think. I don't believe in critical listening, for that only puts a person in a straitjacket of hesitancy. He begins to choose his words solemnly or primly. His little inner fountain cannot spring. Critical listeners dry you up. But creative listeners are those who want you to be recklessly yourself, even at your very worst, even vituperative, bad-tempered. They are laughing and just delighted with any manifestation of yourself, bad or good. For true listeners know that if you are

93

bad-tempered it does not mean that you are always so. They don't love you just when you are nice; they love all of you.

30   If you hold back the
         dull things, you are certain
         to hold back what is clear
         and beautiful too.   30

In order to learn to listen, here are some suggestions: Try to learn tranquility, to live in the present a part of the time every day. Sometimes say to yourself: "Now. What is happening now? This friend is talking. I am quiet. There is endless time. I hear it, every word." Then suddenly you begin to hear not only what people are saying, but what they are trying to say, and you sense the whole truth about them. And you sense existence, not piecemeal, not this object and that, but as a translucent whole.

Then watch your self-assertiveness. And give it up. Try not to drink too many cocktails to give up that nervous pressure that feels like energy and wit but may be neither. And remember it is not enough just to *will* to listen to people. One must *really* listen. Only then does the magic begin.

Sometimes people cannot listen because they think that unless 35 they are talking, they are socially of no account. There are those women with an old-fashioned ballroom training that insists there must be unceasing vivacity and gyrations of talk. But this is really a strain on people.

No. We should all know this: that listening, not talking, is the gifted and great role, and the imaginative role. And the true listener is much more beloved, magnetic than the talker, and he is more effective, and learns more and does more good. And so try listening. Listen to your wife, your husband, your father, your mother, your children, your friends; to those who love you and those who don't, to those who bore you, to your enemies. It will work a small miracle. And perhaps a great one.

BRENDA & CARL

The friendship of two great writers

1 The poet Carl Sandburg had some of his best talks about writ- 1
ing with reporter Brenda Ueland of Minneapolis, a vivacious bru-
nette divorcée whom he met through literary critic Joseph Warren
Beach. In the late '30s when he was in Minneapolis, Sandburg
stayed with Ueland and her family in her big, old house overlooking Lake Calhoun. A sparkling, outspoken woman of Norwegian
heritage, she had lived a bohemian life in Greenwich Village before the First World War, part of the ebullient circle that included
John Reed and Louise Bryant. "I was the first woman in the West-
ern world to have my hair all cut off," she exulted. "I went to
Henri in Greenwich Village . . . and I told him to cut my hair all
off. He was frightened, appalled. To cut off that nice, very black,
ladylike hair, with a pug! It was splendid. Wherever I went seas of
white faces turned to gaze. That is just what I liked."

Despite her avant-garde life-style and her passion for romance
and adventure. Brenda was a purist about love. She and Sandburg
shared a deep attraction, took long walks around the lakeshore
near her home, and talked endlessly about politics and writing.
They shared the constrained, uniquely enriching love between a
man and a woman who could consummate an emotional, spiritual bond physically, but do not. The resulting mutual respect
forged a deep friendship between them, and for years they enjoyed
the electricity of their meetings, in person or in letters.

She and Sandburg talked as they strode around the lake in a
chill Minnesota dusk. Sandburg told Brenda he thought it was
possible for a man to love many women at once, and, perhaps,
impossible for him not to. But, he said vehemently, a commit-
ment to marriage and fidelity to one woman was sacramental. In
her 90s, her black eyes brilliant and fierce, Brenda looked back
on her remarkable life. "I have had many glorious love affairs,"
she smiled, "hundreds of them. But not with Sandburg. We loved
each other, it was true. But never sexually. We chose not to."

Her audacity and honesty endeared her to Sandburg, and he trusted her judgment as a writer, expressing in his letters to her some of his most thoughtful theories about the act of writing. He called her 1938 book *If You Want to Write* (reprint, Graywolf Press) the "best book ever written about how to write."

—Penelope Niven

HOW TO TALK WITH KIDS

Advice to the shapers of the next generation

1 Don't ask your poor children those automatic questions—"Did 1 you wash your hands, dear?"—those dull, automatic, querulous, duty questions (almost the only conversation that most parents have to offer). Note the look of dreadful exhaustion and ennui and boredom that comes into their otherwise quite happy faces. And don't say, "How was school today, dear?" which really means: "Please entertain me (mama) who is mentally totally lazy at the moment with not one witty or interesting thing to offer, and please give me an interesting and stimulating account of high marks."

Years and years ago when my child was 4 years old, I suddenly learned not to do this. I learned—a bolt from Heaven—*never* to ask an automatic question, so boring, so mentally lazy, so exhausting. No, I would *myself* tell *her* something interesting and arresting: "I saw Pat Greaves next door running and bawling because he was being chased by a strange yellow cat." My child's eyes would sparkle with interest, and there we were, in the liveliest conversation, and behold! she was soon telling me the most interesting extraordinary things, her own ideas. At our meals together I felt that it was I, not she, who must be the wit, the raconteur, the delightful one, the fascinated listener to her remarks, the laugher at her jokes. Now, the light in a child's eyes is a splendid gauge and tells you in a split-second if you are failing and becoming a bore and a schoolmarm. She has liked me ever since.

Another aspect of the same thing is this: I say to those young-ish parents (the vast majority these days) who are exhausted by their children and, with pale, neurasthenic frowns on their fore-heads, are always pleading "Plee-ase go to bed, dear . . . Plee-ase now Jack, Sally, Jane, go in the other room dear, and look at tele-vision."

"No," I say, "you are doing it wrong. You are failing as parents. You should be so vigorous, healthy, in the pink of condition (cut out all the smoking and drinking and coffee breaks), so inexhaust-ible, rambunctious, jolly, full of deviltry and frolic, of stories, of dramatizations, of actions, of backward somersaults, or athlet-ics and tomfoolery, of hilarity, that your children at last, after hours of violent exercise, worn down by laughter and intellectual excitement, with pale, neurasthenic frowns on *their* foreheads, cry: "Plee . . . eease, Mama, go to bed!"

—Brenda Ueland

Chapter XIV

How do we attain such a relationship with the world? How do we attain an attitude that is not technological? By recognizing ourselves as Dasein and not the thinking thing, we are in a position to realize that a certain social practice we have allows us to recognize our relationship to Being and, in turn, shows us how to live in response to that relationship. This practice, the central preoccupation of the latter part of Heidegger's life, is...

LANGUAGE

Reprinted from *Heidegger for Beginners*, by Eric Lemay and Jennifer A. Pitts, illustrated by Paul Gordon (1994), For Beginners LLC.

Through our language we have a way of experiencing our original relationship with the mystery of existence.

Language is something like an extended memory for Being, which records all the moments when beings come into existence.

Every historical appearance of Being creates a special word which then becomes a symbol of that appearance.

If we trace our most fundamental words back to their origins, we can recall the original experience of their coming into existence through Being.

The following example helps illustrate the primordial significance Heidegger gave to language. Take the word "love" as it is used today in our society.

LANGUAGE OF LOVE TAKE #2

PLEASE GET OUT OF THE WAY, I LOVE YOU.

NO, YOU DON'T. YOU DON'T KNOW WHAT LOVE MEANS. YESTERDAY YOU SAID YOU "LOVE HOCKEY" AND "LOVE BEER." BESIDES, YOU'RE JUST SAYING THAT BECAUSE BOWLING WAS CANCELLED AND YOU WANT TO WATCH TV. WELL, WE'RE GOING BALLROOM DANCING.

After seeing the word "Love" used on thousands of greeting cards, soap commercials, movie reviews and tie-dye tee shirts, the word has become impoverished. "Love" no longer carries the meaning and significance it once did. Today, saying "I love you" is not much different from saying "Pass the salt."

I love you!

ROCKY XII

"I LOVED IT!"

Heidegger thought that this process of words becoming impoverished took place over a long period of time. Each generation adds another layer of crud over the original meaning of a word, covering it like layers of rust. To follow Heidegger's view, there was a moment in time when someone first used the word "love."

At this moment there was no difference between the word and its meaning, between the word and the untainted experience of it. "Love" came into existence at the moment it was spoken. In that very instant, the being called "love" came into existence through Being.

"*i love you*"

For Heidegger, the key to understanding our place in the world comes from recognizing the initial moment of existence, the moment "Being speaks," that lies at the center of our most important words. By uncovering all the layers of rust that history has placed over the original experience of the words central to our lives—truth, knowledge, human, etc.,—we can once again live in regard to these events of existence.

So, for example, when someone says, **"I love you,"** they will experience the true and original significance of their words and, consequently, act in a manner which accepts the responsibility for such an utterance.

The original experience of most of the words central to our lives are embedded in the Greek language. According to Heidegger, the Greek language is no ordinary language but rather one with a special and immanent relationship to Being.

THIS IS THE GREEK TONGUE. IT HAS A VERY SPECIAL RELATIONSHIP TO BEING.

IN THE GREEK LANGUAGE, WHAT IS SAID, _IS_ AT THE SAME TIME.

Our fundamental words come into existence through Being in the Greek language, a language in which those fundamental questions were first voiced. Due to the language's special relationship to beings and Being, Heidegger stated that Greek was the **_Logos:_** a language where the words of the language are inseparable from what they name.

HELLO!

HELLO!

HOW ARE YOU?

...RE YOU?

HOMER, WHY THE DOUBLE TALK? YOU'RE GREEK!

In order to uncover and experience our most important words, we have to trace them back to their original existence in Greek. Once we have done this, we can begin to understand our relationship with Being.

MR. HEIDEGGER, WOULD YOU EXPLAIN TO US THE MEANING OF BEING?

IT'S ALL GREEK TO ME...

Our entire language, the language of *Dasein*, becomes the living memory of beings coming into existence or, as Heidegger put it, **"Language is the house of Being."** We are that special being who can ask questions about Being and, having that ability, we become the keepers or guardians of Being.

Appendix

Like much of what we talked about in this book, writing a paper is engaging with a process. Most people approach writing a paper as a product. This assignment asks you to shift your point-of-view. Do not aim at the A or what I, the professor, want but instead use the assignment to do your own thinking. The paper is called a think paper because I am asking that you think. This is not a book report where you tell me what the book is about but rather a place to integrate how everything is coming together for you this semester.

First, the paper needs to answer three questions: 1) how are you making sense of the class?, 2) how are the readings helping you to make sense of the class?, 3) how the readings and the class connected to your life? In other words, I am asking you to integrate experience, theory (to see), and application in this paper. I also ask that you write the entire paper in first person. We are learning that using the language of "I" is the language of responsibility. This is not a research paper where you tell me what others think. Here, you have an opportunity to tell me what you think. Remember, to think does not mean you focus on like/dislike, agree/disagree, etc.. I do not care about those things. That which I am most interested in is your ability to generate thought.

This is where you take what you have learned and make it your own (breathe new life into it).

Second, some questions that you may ask yourself in preparation for writing the paper are: 1) Has there been a change since the beginning of the semester? Have you noticed a change in yourself? If so, what is it? If not, why not? 2) What do you think is the most important idea for you this semester? Which idea do you keep coming back to or helps you understand something?

Third, I will outline a process for uncovering a topic if you do not immediately arrive at one:
   a) review reflections you wrote after each class
   b) try to distill each reflection into one word
   c) make a list of the words
   d) look for a theme in the words
   e) if there is a theme, this could be your topic
   f) try to form the topic into a thesis sentence. This is the most important part of the paper. Before you start to write, you need to know the thesis since the entire paper supports the thesis.
   g) write an outline
   h) write a draft of the paper
   i) revise the draft into the final paper

Fourth, if you do not have a direction you can just start writing. Remember that what you write is not the paper. It is the process that you are entering to figure out what you want to write about. People who teach writing say that one way around writer's block is to start writing. The movement of the hand connects with the movement of the mind. This connects back to the ancient Greek idea that thinking and learning required movement. Sometimes you can use the activity of writing to figure out what you wish to say. Frequently, people come to the point they wish to make at the end of the writing exercise. If that happens for you, start the paper over with the end at the beginning. The concluding point is now the thesis. You can now write the outline. Preparation of an outline works on making sure all the organizational issues are worked out before you set out to write.

OUTLINE FORMAT

Introduction
I. Attention getter
II. General approach to the topic
III. Thesis statement
IV. Preview of main points
(transition)

Body
I. First main point
a) supporting material
b) supporting material
c) supporting material
(transition)

II. Second main point
a) supporting material
b) supporting material
c) supporting material
(transition)

III. Third main point
a) supporting material
b).supporting material
c) supporting material
(transition)

Conclusion
I. Restate thesis
II. Review main points
III. Closure

Come up with the thesis first and then go back to see how you need to introduce the thesis.

Bibliography

Adler, Ronald B., Lawrence B. Rosenfeld and Russell F. Proctor II. *Interplay: The Process of Interpersonal Communication.* New York: Oxford University Press, 2010.

Doidge, Norman. *The Brain that Changes Itself.* New York: Viking Press, 2007.

Farrell Leontiou, Janet. *What Do The Doctors Say: How Doctors Create a World through Their Words.* Bloomington, IN: iUniverse, 2010

Frankl, Viktor E. *Man's Search for Meaning.* New York: Simon & Schuster, 1959.

_____. *The Doctor and the Soul.* New York: Vintage Books, 1986.

Gadamer, Hans-George. *Truth and Method.* New York: Crossroad Publishing, 1975.

Lakoff, Robin. *Language and Woman's Place.* New York: Harper & Row, 1975.

Postman, Neil. *Amusing Ourselves to Death: Public Discourse in the Age of Show Business.* New York: Penguin Books, 1985.

Rosenfield, Lawrence W. and Janet Farrell Leontiou. "Museus e Magazines: The Art of Display" edited by A.M. Barbosa in *Congreso Nationale de Pesquisadoires em Artes Plasticas,* Anais 96, vo. I, 1997.

Rosenthal, Robert and Lenore Jacobson. *Pygmalion in the Class-room.* New York: Irvington Press, 1992.

Tannen, Deborah. *You Just Don't Understand: Men and Women in Conversation.* New York: HarperCollins, 2001.